Fifty Years of
Indian Management

FIFTY YEARS OF
INDIAN MANAGEMENT

An Insider's View

ARABINDA RAY

OXFORD
UNIVERSITY PRESS

OXFORD
UNIVERSITY PRESS

YMCA Library Building, Jai Singh Road, New Delhi 110001

Oxford University Press is a department of the University of Oxford. It furthers the
University's objective of excellence in research, scholarship, and education
by publishing worldwide in

Oxford   New York
Athens   Auckland   Bangkok   Bogota   Buenos Aires   Calcutta
Cape Town   Chennai   Dar es Salaam   Delhi   Florence   Hong Kong   Istanbul
Karachi   Kuala Lumpur   Madrid   Melbourne   Mexico City   Mumbai
Nairobi   Paris   Sao Paolo   Singapore   Taipei   Tokyo   Toronto   Warsaw

with associated companies in

Berlin   Ibadan

ISBN 0 19 565123 5

Typeset by Eleven Arts, Keshav Puram, Delhi 110 035
Printed in India by Saurabh Print-O-Pack, Noida,
and published by Manzar Khan, Oxford University Press
YMCA Library Building, Jai Singh Road, New Delhi 110 001

Dedicated to
Sir James Lindsay
and
Prakash Tandon

two great pioneers in the professionalization of
management in independent India

Preface

Fifty years is a long time for the history of management in any country—more so in India which had no background of an industrial revolution and where the practice of clocktime adherence developed only one hundred years or so before Independence. On the other hand we have had the advantage of acquiring or discarding practices and systems which had evolved naturally over many years in the industrially advanced countries. As in many other spheres in India, such acquisition was piecemeal and variously selective so that we have a spectrum beginning at one end with archaic systems and practices and having at the other end highly sophisticated management which can compare with the most advanced in any country.

Nearly three decades ago when India's first generation managers had not seriously looked at themselves, Dr Kamla Chaudhuri, an eminent teacher of management at the time, encouraged me to write about my experience of being a first generation manager. She complained that we were all looking far too much at Western personalia and were leaving scant records of personal impressions for a later day historian to understand the processes through which Indian management was developing. However insignificant one may feel in the totality of the profession, each perspective had something to contribute to the understanding of the totality.

I was reminded of Woodruff's classic, *The Men Who Ruled India*—the history of two hundred years of British rule in India seen from the perspective of an administrator in each decade. In a moving preface Woodruff said in 1954 when his book was first published that whilst it was still too early for anybody to write an authoritative assessment of the British period in Indian history, there were many things which needed to be put down by those like himself about their experiences before they were forgotten.

Dr Chaudhuri's efforts resulted in a series of essays in the *Economic and Political Weekly* which the *Weekly* later in 1970 brought out in book form under the title *The Indian Manager in Search of a Style*. Despite trepidations, the book did receive a great deal of notice, justifying Dr Chaudhuri's belief about the need for such personal recording.

In writing that book I believed that practising managers like myself at the time needed to be aware of the parametres —historical, sociological, and national—within which we operated. We needed, in the light of that awareness, to discover not just the limitations but the immense scope within our powers to attain the fulfilment of the promises inherent in our types. Each had to make the discovery for himself; I had no new knowledge or learning to offer, but if after reading that book any manager operating in India was influenced merely to look at his profession self-consciously, it would be ample reward for me.

Now three decades later I am well into retirement. In today's world obsolescence can be very rapid. However, having initiated something thirty years ago which struck many chords, I felt I owed it to myself—once again before memory faded—to go through fifty eventful years in the development of the Indian manager from purely personal experience. This is no knowledgeable or even responsible recording of history: it does not follow chronology or quote authoritative commentators. It is, instead, a personal view of how the process unfolded, the upsurges and drags, the achievements and failures, and finally, just to take recourse to jargon without which nothing seems to be conclusive in management writing, a collective SWOT analysis.

I make no claims that my views are incontrovertible, but would like them to be regarded as a possible way of looking at issues. If this book assists many others to write about their own experiences, if the new generations oblivious of their history finding current happenings inaccurately portrayed write to protest, my purpose will have been served.

In an age when the country is battling fissiparous forces, the pan-Indianism of the management world is a welcome beacon of light. There do not seem too many dangers of the former tendencies striking a chord in the management world, but one needs to be ever-cautious since after all managers are members of society and do not operate in a vacuum.

Fifty years is a long time to have been associated with a way of life. Before one leaves it all behind, it gives a great deal of satisfaction to have overviewed that period from one's own experience.

Contents

ONE

The Advent of Professional
Management in India

It is important to begin by defining the term 'manager'
for the purpose of the present exercise and to distin-
guish the manager from the 'entrepreneur'. Quite a lot
of management literature deals essentially with the capitalist's role as opposed to the function of pure management as
such. In many instances the entrepreneur is, of course, also
a manager in the sense that I use the term here; but the
scene from which this survey begins—the era commencing
from the first Industrial Policy Resolution of independent
India in 1948—had not seen the emergence of the manager
as a class by itself.

The entrepreneur sets out to exploit opportunities he sees
in a certain sphere and employs his capital. His stakes are,
therefore, closely bound with an efficient return on capital.
His decision to stay or move away from the business is
governed by his assessment of the return on his capital.
The entrepreneur employs the manager to make possible
the most effective utilization of resources: not just in a static
sense to derive the best out of a given situation, but in a

manner which will not only not jeopardize the possibilities of such or more effective utilization in the future, but will on the contrary increase such possibilities. The resources that the manager has to command and direct are multi-dimensional and as one progresses higher up the ladder of managerial success, one is increasingly dealing with a greater number of dimensions, and the job requirement changes from the ability to use knowledge to the skill in getting subordinates to apply their knowledge in a manner orchestrated by oneself.

Modern commerce and industry began to make an appearance in India from the middle of the nineteenth century—at first through commercial dealings in foreign, notably British, houses; and then with enterprising Indian businessmen who were rapidly shedding the role of pure compradors. Even so, as recently as 1933, of the twenty top business houses in India, seventeen were British, most of them based in Calcutta. Amongst the three Indian houses, Tatas was the most respected, Birla had just joined the set, and Currimbhoy of Bombay was on its way out.

From the middle of the nineteenth century, trading houses turned to organized industry, which began to make its appearance—under British capital in the east and under Indian capital in the west. Coalmining, tea plantation, jute and cotton mills begin in this period. The industrial unit was still a small one by today's standards. It was consequently possible to find the required capital from within the family or from a group of friends and, since the scale of industry was not large, problems of management—of labour and of raw material—were relatively simple.

Management during this period was characterized by three principal features. First, the entrepreneurial and managerial functions were not segregated; second, there was considerable reliance on family members in the case of Indian businessmen and on expatriates—with suitable introductions from home—in foreign firms for managerial services; and third, business had considerable operational flexibility to withstand changing situations. Where devolution of functions did take place it was restricted to such family members; this devolution took place mostly in respect of selling, purchasing, and man management. In all these respects, a family member or highly trusted retainer was accepted and considered suitable proxy in management for the entrepreneur. For example, in the managing agency system (the predominant method of managing a diverse group of trading and manufacturing activities adopted by both British and Indian business houses), the key positions in the agency company were held in the case of British agencies by expatriates and in Indian agencies by family members; in the managed companies or divisions, outsiders carried out day-to-day activities.

However, this observation does not hold true for technical functions. As far as these were concerned—in a textile mill, coalmine, or ship-repairing works—a clear policy of hiring from the market was followed on the basis of technical requirements, but as far as non-technical functions were concerned, the habits derived from trading enterprises were continued. These functions were deemed to be a family preserve and were allocated on the basis of family connections and convenience. The instrument which made such family control of management possible across the board was the managing agency system which for a long time enjoyed the existence of scant legal provisions governing the management of enterprises. Only through the 1936 amendment of the Companies Act was effective control first exercised.

Our period of fifty years effectively begins from the enunciation of the Industrial Policy Resolution in 1948. By this time the growth of Indian industry was reaching a stage where the deployment of professional management was becoming unavoidable. The major impact on the management system arose from the formalization of institutional controls. The post World War I period saw the emergence of strong competition marked by a major depression in the industrially advanced countries. Indian industry had to be highly competitive if it was to survive. Where, for various reasons, it was not sufficiently competitive it could seek tariff protection then being established by the government. The tariff system introduced industry to a formal costing system since the need for tariff protection had to be proved with convincing figures before an independent body of experts. For the first time costs began to be examined independently and not just as an item to be differentiated from total revenue to arrive at a profit figure. By the same token, to get round the tariff protection and also take advantage of it, foreign companies began to set up branches or subsidiary operations in India. They enjoyed at the time complete freedom in the percentage of foreign capital participation or employment of foreign personnel. At the same time they brought their management practices with them and trained a number of local personnel in current management techniques and positions thus began to be open to people other than those belonging to entrepreneural families.

This expansion of activity resulted in the managing agency becoming a diversified enterprise (a conglomerate in today's parlance) covering a broad range of industries.

Entry into each new industry involved knowledge of its specific problems: need to draw management talent from outside, therefore, also became necessary. In the first instance the Indian managing agencies looked within the family as far as possible to find the right people, but for both British and Indian entrepreneurs each expansion generally meant an overload at the top. This dependence on family members in the case of Indian companies often had the later day unfortunate result of divisions due to family frictions or the harbouring of ineffective managerial personnel.

Then came the sea change during and in the wake of World War II which ushered in a continuous process of application of newer and newer technology. As Galbraith has said, technology means the systematic application of scientific knowledge to practical tasks and its most important consequence is enforcing the division and subdivision of any such task into its component parts. Division of a task into several parts and specialization at each stage requires knowledge and, more importantly, meaningful organizational coordination, to give worthwhile total results. Professional management as we understand it today, in its essence consists of that crucial ability to find the interconnecting link between apparently disparate objects and in a relevant practical situation using the linking factor effectively.

The stage was thus set for the professional manager to step into the Indian scene. At the end of World War II there was widespread appreciation of the fact that management of logistics, industries, and diversities of personnel required specialized handling. At the same time, the wave of management education originating in America and already beginning to influence Britain started reaching Indian shores. Expatriates and Indians returning from Harvard or Henley spread the message that there was a lot in professional management for which one could not rely on experience alone but had to go back to the classroom.

It is to the credit of the government of the time that there was immediate appreciation of the need for treating professional management as an item of formal training and knowledge acquisition. More than that, there was the important realization that, as in many other spheres, in independent India we had to achieve in a decade—by deliberate, planned, boot-strap-lifting operation—what had been achieved in the West through natural evolution of more than a century.

The discussion, henceforth, will be on the way this job was tackled, and where it has brought us today: the successes and the mistakes, the omissions and obstacles.

Even at the beginning of our period there was certainly a clutch of very competent managers on the scene but given the state of industry at the time and the nature of corporate ownership, there was understandably a limited number of true professionals as the word has come to mean since. Nevertheless, one cannot ignore the high quality of management in the service sector—such as the railways, postal services, and ports—which in every way met the demands of the modern definition of professional management. It is a pity that their success did not open the doors of the corporate sector earlier to the Indian middle class. Trade and industry were dominated by large family concerns who owed little accountability to the public or even to their shareholders; there were of course large foreign, mostly British, concerns which almost exclusively used their own countrymen in top managerial positions. It is also true that there were major Indian houses like the Tatas and there was strong Indian presence in the field of banking and in the textile mills in western India. But, by and large, the number of managers employed, as opposed to senior technical experts, was limited.

The process began with the continuation of the easy pace of agency type businesses. Gradually came the adaptation to local circumstances. As with other areas where India was catching up with the rest of the world, it relied heavily on formal education both at pre-experience and post-experience levels. India has never been short of academic talent. When, therefore, world management began to be heavily influenced by information technology, it came into its own by jumping gaps and catching up with the advanced pack. The spectrum continues to be as broad as before but within it there is a perceptible increase in the progressive band.

TWO

Choosing a New Career

There was up to the time little motivation or incentive amongst the educated elite to look to management as a career. First of all there was no awareness of the existence of a useful career as such in this field; but, more importantly, the value system of Indian society did not encourage members of the elite or the upper middle class to look at a career in trade or industry. India was the meeting ground of two of the most class conscious cultures the world has ever seen. Hindu society gave pride of place to academia (Brahmanism) and the Kshatriya culture of landholding and valour; management was to be associated with Vaisya values and had little social respectability. At the same time Victorian Britain gave pre-eminence to the administrator and the soldier in its colonial society barely suffering the trader as an unavoidable evil. Membership to the high society exclusive clubs of British India was restricted to senior administrators and army personnel and there were embargos on the commercial types. Even in Muslim India trade was left in the hands of Hindus whilst the Muslim members of high society concentrated on governance and warfare.

An incident, amusing today but quite serious at the time it occurred in the late thirties, highlights this cultural bias. An astrologer was preparing the horoscopes of all the members of a very well-established Bengal family which boasted top lawyers and doctors, highly placed civil servants, and Oxbridge returned academics. For the family's most precocious member, then 8 years old, he forecast a job with a fixed salary—a common description of the remuneration of those who worked in business organization and banks—casting the whole family in deep gloom. Nobody could, however, explain to the puzzled boy precisely what 'fixed salary' meant. He asked his uncle, a professor, whether the term did not include him as well with his salaried job. The uncle was appalled. Whether the astrologer was proficient or not, the boy in question was the first from the family, some thirteen years later, to join a multinational firm as trainee and rise to be a Board member in his mid-thirties. In his forties he went on to other top management jobs in India. By that time, of course, the business manager was highly acclaimed in the same Bengali society.

One area where India traditionally employed professional managers was estate management. Unfortunately, the net record of landowners and their managers was such that the zamindari system was axed soon after Independence. The opportunity of taking an area where there was accumulated expertise and modernizing it in stages was thus lost. It is generally believed that the promulgation of the Permanent Settlement by Lord Cornwallis in the northern territories of the East India Company in 1793 created a class of wealthy landlords who, as time went on, used their considerable earnings from the land in leading lives of leisure in the cities. Only in rare instances as with Dwarkanath Tagore—the poet's grandfather—was that wealth diverted into trading, coalmining, manufacturing, and commercial service activities like banking and steamships. Even rarer was the case of a visionary landlord who would use his estates for scientific cultivation and encourage the *ryots* with developmental rebates on their payable taxes. Had this example of a progressive landlord like Joykissen Mookherjee of Uttarpara in Bengal been extensively followed, then the zamindari system would not have fallen into general disrepute and raised political opposition which led to it being abolished. With the advent of modernity, the managing of an estate without being an owner would have certainly developed into a career in every sense of modern professional management. In England, for example, leading universities offer courses in estate management. The success of plantation managers in India leaves no doubt that management of sizable rice, wheat, or sugarcane producing estates could have been similarly professionalized along with other aspects of real estate management. Although tyrannical real estate managers are a common theme in Indian language fiction there are many instances of able, enlightened *dewans, naibs,* or paid managers who understood what it took to develop agricultural property. It has to be said that twentieth-century India lost, through the ineptitude of pre-independence landowners as a class, the opportunity of creating a major avenue of professional management where the country's middle classes might have been gainfully employed.

From backgrounds of law, medicine, landholding, teaching, government service, and, hardly ever, business, first-generation managers, unprepared by their backgrounds, began to enter the corporate sector in significant numbers from about fifty years ago. What induced them to do so? In the first place, openings were becoming more easily available. British firms, notably the managing agencies, were trying to adapt themselves to the changed political situation by admitting Indians, however grudgingly, to the so-called 'covenanted' positions which theoretically approximated the conditions of service of expatriates. But the percentages were still very low: the expatriate was generally well protected in the hierarchy and rarely, if at all, placed under an Indian senior. The men chosen came from a background of good connections and anglicized education; academic excellence was not only not required but actually frowned upon. Skill at games, attendance at certain well-known boarding schools, and military backgrounds (provided by a recently concluded global war) had almost exclusive premium. A defiant Indian executive working in an MNC in the engineering sector, when asked at a party in the early sixties if he had taken to golf retorted, 'Why should I? I am doing well enough on my job as it is, thank you'!

In 1957, Mr T.T. Krishnamachari, then Minister of Commerce and Industry, was under pressure to step up the rate of Indianization of executive staff in foreign-owned private sector companies. Next door in Pakistan there had been official instructions to get the number up to 50 per cent within a short span of time. In conformity with India's generally tolerant policies, T.T.K. did not fix quotas or talk of legislation but introduced a system of six-monthly returns, which all foreign-owned and managed companies in India had to submit, to indicate the progress in Indianization of executive staff. However, as proof of the general ignorance of what was really happening in that sector the threshold was fixed at Rs 500 per month which, even allowing for lower costs at the time and the lack of precise definition of what 'salary' constituted, naturally inflated the Indian percentage, although the higher echelons remained unattainable to Indians. The overall statistics, therefore, showed a fair percentage of Indian executives although even with this definition it hardly ever exceeded 20 per cent. This system of returns was given up within a period of two to three years. However, it was not till the devaluation of the Indian rupee in 1966 that management in India saw large scale exodus of British and American expatriates who could no longer save enough pounds or dollars from their Indian earnings.

Since the managing agency was at the time the principal source of employment for managers and managing agencies were largely concentrated in the then commercial capital, Calcutta, and were essentially British owned, it may not be out of place to give some pictures of the lifestyle of the executive world in British-dominated managing agencies.

Dress at work was, of course, formal as it was then in many other spheres: a jacket and a tie were *de jure*, but on half-day Saturdays the jacket was dispensable. Since offices were not airconditioned it was permissible to take the jacket off, but as hierarchy was deeply respected it was to be donned if called by a superior. Lunch was served in the multi-tiered office dining rooms (if not multi-tiered by chambers at least by tables and timings) but convention existed that on Friday afternoons one, if senior enough, would go to Firpo's or the club for an extended lunch, returning to office well after three o'clock. This practice had its origin in the fact that one had worked hard during the week to send off the weekly report to London office by Friday's midday post to catch the boat train mail in Bombay on time and was entitled to a diversion. The 'diversion' was still necessary in the days when the boat train had been replaced by daily airmail!

The unity of this restricted corporate world was at its best outside work. The managing agency world had a busy social programme, especially in the cooler months. However, even socializing was layered. *Chhokras* had their own fun, usually of a rumbustious nature, while their seniors wore black ties almost every day of the week to attend a cocktail party or dinner. On Fridays and Saturdays, the clans would congregate at some of the several night clubs which provided live bands and floor shows—Maxim, Prince's, the Golden Slipper, and the Three Hundred Club (the last named being for the more elevated personnel). The late night film shows in the then well-appointed airconditioned cinema halls with their elegant brasserie bars for the interval were popular haunts after a cocktail party or an early supper. Ambitious young aspirants began dressing with black ties for late night film shows to give a favourable impression to a boss likely to be there as if he had also come from a cocktail party! Vikram Seth's *A Suitable Boy* gives vivid sketches of this lifestyle.

Social clubs were very exclusive and again striated not just racially. The Bengal Club was for the seniors and tended to look down on jute mill managers and non-public school types. The Saturday Club was one which young expatriates with public school backgrounds joined immediately on arrival. Even in 1955, a senior Works Manager from Yorkshire of a large engineering company was not admitted into the Saturday Club because he had no acceptable background and had worked his way up in Calcutta. Indians working in agencies in 'covenanted' positions presumably had good 'class background' and, if there was not an overall racial bar, qualified for membership.

The managing agency culture was so dominant even in the sporting clubs that an Indian executive from an engineering firm had to be formally 'interviewed' by the committee although he had grown up with most of the committee members—a practice not followed by the club in respect of entrants from managing agencies.

Sport was very prominent amongst corporate executives —mainly golf, riding, shooting, tennis, squash, rowing, and cricket. Younger executives played in office football, hockey, and cricket teams. However, just to show the extent to which managing agencies dominated this world as well, the Merchants' Cup Golf Competition—a major event in Calcutta's business world—in its rules up to the fifties, restricted entry to those who had their offices in the old area of Calcutta town under the direct jurisdiction of the High Court and proscribed players from the Company's mills and factories in the suburbs of Calcutta.

Many such practices, anachronistic in terms of today's values, could be described. However, there was one very positive training aspect. The long six-months' furlough which executives enjoyed after every three years' work gave an opportunity to the juniors to stand in and gain experience. It also gave the discerning executive an opportunity to look at new developments abroad.

Corporate life in the few Indian managing agencies that existed was much more serious and work-dominated by contrast. Salaries also did not match at the junior to middle level. There was little socializing outside work. Since family members for whom retirement provisions did not apply generally occupied the top positions indefinitely, career progress was slow; if the equation between the boss and his executive was good even diagonal shifting did not take place. Not unnaturally, therefore, there was a good deal of envy for their counterparts in foreign agencies.

THREE

Educating the Professionals

The first task in transition was from administrator to business manager. Indians' acknowledged strength in administration had to be reshaped and this is where the bridge was provided by the heavy dosage of management education. We have had to grapple in this context with all the handicaps of the management of public sector undertakings where, unhappily, the bureaucratic culture has held a firm grip. It is a sign of maturity of the country's decision-makers and enterprise managers that despite political opposition this vicious control is surely, if slowly, being dismantled. It is also a tribute to Indian management as a whole that the early pioneers and their successors were able to establish a profession not traditionally accepted in a status-conscious society in a pre-eminent position.

Entrants to management began mustering numbers with the stimulus to industrialization beginning from the early fifties. Factories and plantations, it was always agreed, required technical personnel but the realization was beginning to dawn that the management as such of enterprises in the changing world required special skills which were capable of being developed in an accelerated way with training. Experience of the conduct of a modern war heavily dependent on the quality of management of men and logistics had shown the way. The country had been exposed to American influences where business administration was already a well-established curriculum subject in leading universities and for the first time more Indian students going overseas were proceeding to the USA in comparison to Britain.

In all new movements a core group of pioneers set the path. In India, too, certain enlightened industry personnel, Indian and British, started a management movement with the setting up of management associations. The Calcutta Management Association was not founded till 1958, but a Senior Management Course was run by some enthusiastic Henley-returned Indian and British managers in the city with the help of the West Bengal government annually from 1956, under the title of 'Ad Hoc Management Development Programme'. This was later formalized into an annual three-week residential programme which the Calcutta Management Association ran in Puri or Ranchi. Likewise, the Bombay Management Association and the Madras Institute of Management (later re-named Madras Management Association) had come into being slightly earlier. These were initially discussion groups under different disciplines like marketing, finance, and production, where members exchanged experiences, studied foreign practices, and got eminent businessmen and bureaucrats in the city or passing through it to deliver lectures and run short-term training programmes. In the restricted community of corporate executives it became a status symbol for young executives to have been sent to a management course by the employer or to be seen in management association gatherings.

Looking back at that period one is astonished at the rapid inroads professional management made in government and corporate estimation. As early as the mid-fifties, the central government and some of the state governments had accepted the need for formal management education. The Administrative Staff College of India (ASCI) at Hyderabad was functional from 1956 and the two Indian Institutes of Management at Calcutta and Ahmedabad were going concerns by 1962. Locally, at several leading universities embryonic or full-fledged management schools or departments were coming into existence.

The All India Management Association (AIMA) came into being as a kind of apex body to promote the formation of activities of local management associations in 1957. As far as direct university-level formal management education is concerned, the first institution was set up in Calcutta as early as 1954, under the leadership of Dr B.C.Roy and with the support of the topmost British and Indian businessmen in the city at the time (All India Institute of Social Welfare and Business Management, since re-christened Indian Institute of Social Welfare and Business Management or IISWBM). Andhra University and the Jamnalal Bajaj Institute in Bombay followed soon after. Both these were autonomous institutions, offering a final examination under the aegis of the local university.

Planning on the Indian Institutes of Management (IIM) at Calcutta and Ahmedabad in academic collaboration with MIT and Harvard respectively, started from 1960. They were fully operational by 1965 and became the ultimate management training institutes. IIMs were later, in the seventies and eighties, extended to Bangalore, Lucknow, and now to Indore and Calicut. In Jamshedpur, the Xavier Labour Relations Institute (XLRI), specializing initially in personnel management, became, through the seventies, a respected general management training institute. The Industrial Finance Corporation of India (IFCI) set up a well-staffed institute near Delhi in the late seventies. Others—with international support—kept coming up through the eighties and nineties. All these institutions maintained a close liaison with corporate management and received considerable corporate sponsorship in their executive development programmes and capital projects.

At the end of the century, a stage has been reached when an MBA is a prized acquisition of a young Indian especially if it is from one of the IIMs. The all India Common Admission Tests every year attract thousands of meritorious students. It is fairly common to find young persons who have already spent a considerable number of years acquiring an engineering degree or a professional competence in accountancy, law, or even medicine, hankering after an MBA degree for advancement in life. In a later chapter the implications of this will be discussed.

In the beginning, the new recruits into managerial careers from such institutions were coming into job situations with pre-experience formal training which their superiors had not been exposed to. This was inevitably a source of conflict leading to ineffective utilization of young talent; at the same time, there was not a unnatural impudence in the young recruits vis-á-vis their managers who, by and large, did not possess the same degree of academic attainment. This was a pity because this hiatus prevented the young men from respecting the valuable experience of their seniors and learning from it. Progressive organizations assessed this problem and took care of it by sending their established managers to staff colleges in India and abroad and other appropriate training programmes; but the real solution to the problem necessarily had to await there being in position a continuous spectrum of management with similar attainments. This process—inevitably time-consuming—was unavoidable for the induction of first generation managers. But today, when we are dealing with the third or fourth generation manager who has grown up in a managerial ambience unlike his forebears we probably need to reassess the relative importance of pre-experience and post-experience formal management education.

The situation was analogous to that great meritocracy-based career path which was the dream of the colonial Indian. Years ago, the Indian Civil Service (ICS) had built up a superb tradition of selection which almost pre-determined success on the job by concentrating on the academic excellence of an aspirant and developing the requisite competence on the job through training. When the new appointee, with his brilliant academic record and an Oxbridge rounding-off, went to serve in a district he could not but look up to the officer under whom he would serve because the latter had the same academic record and between fifteen and twenty years of priceless experience which the new recruit could never match.

Not so with the first generation of managers coming in with a great deal of pre-experience education. Their antipathy to not so academically advanced seniors was a cause of personal frustration but they failed in another direction. In a society where age and seniority had been synonymous for long, the superceded oldtimers searched for qualities in these recruits which had given these men such a lead in life. Once again, social conventions had prepared them to accept, grudgingly, the fact that those coming from 'highly placed' families or sons of people with influential jobs which impinged on their employers' organizations would have such leads. But when boys from the same middle class families from which they came, who often had similar school and college educations as their own sons, began entering as 'management trainees' soon moving into executive positions by virtue of their MBAs, they wanted to understand how exactly this education contributed to such advancement. To a certain extent they were impressed with the self-confidence of the young men, the easy familiarity they established with their own bosses, but they rarely found direct evidence of their superior education in their own spheres of work. It took time for this new generation to accept that their role was to build on the skills of their men and coordinate these skills to the organization's best advantage. The chartered accountant had to use his academic knowledge, not just to increase the routine efficiency of the senior accounts clerk of twenty-year standing, but to show him entirely new horizons of the use to which accountancy could be put in the running of the organization; the new graduate engineer could never teach the skilled craftsman how to do his job better, but if he had to earn the right to lead the craftsman he had to display competence in process or product design, the use of new materials, and predetermining results by theoretical calculation; the graduate from the marketing stream of a management school could not hope to teach a salesman how to sell better in the field, but he could bring in planning, market research, and forecasting with relevant practical results.

With the setting up of management schools there began wide appreciation of the fact that modern management required a set of knowledge which was best acquired through formal post-graduate education and needed to be continuously refreshed. Up to this time the entrants to managerial positions were there because they found the remunerations and perquisites attractive and were not prepared to face up to the demands of higher studies. With the cream of Indian universities (who did not or could not go abroad) the professions of medicine, law, and engineering still held sway and even the diminution of the ICS into the IAS (Indian Administrative Service) did not dampen the enthusiasm of meritorious to prepare for the arduous entrance examinations. The current craze for MBAs amongst toppers was still to come. Above anything else, the MBA route demonstrated that entry into managerial positions did not necessarily require pull and influence.

But one of the leading attractions of managerial jobs at the time was also the example of those who had been fortunate enough to get in the early fifties. Trade and industry had grown so fast and the invasion of expatriates been so controlled (largely on grounds of cost) that those early entrants generally had spectacular career growths in early life. In a society dominated by standards of age-revered bureaucratic advancement the fact of young men in their thirties being able to afford distinctly high standards of living was a revelation. By the end of the fifties it was beginning to be accepted in India that the management of modern business required a certain amount of academic and intellectual acumen. As the syllabus of management education began to get more and more sophisticated, management was beginning to acquire an aura of professionalism. Whether what was being taught in such management education programmes was, in fact, being applied in practice at work is another matter, but it was enough that the profession was seen and believed to be knowledge based. It was not till the eighties that theoretical management education, particularly in the field of finance and quantitative techniques, began to be actually applied within organizations largely assisted by the arrival on the scene of computers. By this time professional management was already a highly prized career and men capable of absorbing the new sophisticated knowledge were abundantly available within its ambit.

The perceived affluence of the successful young manager had its problems as well. Friends in other spheres and old college mates who worked in the government did not take kindly to the gulf that separated their respective lifestyles. Understandably, they sought consolation in the presumed importance of their own careers in the nation-building context and were scornful of their 'merchant' friends' interest in serious topics and national policies even though the latter may have had better academic records when they were students together. Halfway through the period and emphatically through the eighties and nineties, the business manager has been able to establish himself as an intellectual equal in a society where he was looked at almost contemptuously in the sixties. Successive governments' economic moguls now consult industry managers before formulating any policy. This itself is eloquent testimony to the arrival of Indian professional management.

FOUR

Conflicts

T he foregoing chapters emphasize the fact that the development of Indian management is a fairly recent process and that, as with many other aspects of life in modern India, the natural processes of its evolution had necessarily to be severely compressed; in the beginning book learning had to substitute genetic and environmental experience. Since the entrants into the world of management were, in those early cases, from families and backgrounds not only unfamiliar with business but often derisive of business careers, they had necessarily to fall back on academic inputs to cope with the growing complexities of management in a world with which they were unfamiliar by upbringing.

They also had to resolve in their own minds the acquired antipathy towards business which existed in the family: having grown up in an India fighting to throw off the British yoke, young persons found themselves giving the best of their time and talent to serving British masters and helping British wealth to grow. A sense of pioneering pride in the

the country's economic growth provided the compromising salve to the sensitive mind—even when promoting the sale of tobacco or soap.

Not only was business coming into India at a pace and in a variety hitherto unmatched, but the very nature of the management of enterprises and the growing existence of imponderables were making the acquisition of new knowledge and techniques indispensable. Jawaharlal Nehru's observation about the process of development in India is very apt in the context of Indian management: Participants had to begin to run before they had even learned to walk.

In the beginning, most of the management material was derived from the Western world and was often not practically relevant to India. It would take at least three decades for Indian course materials to be available but by that time second and third generation managers were being trained.

In those early days, the literature of a free market economy, of a homogeneous and basically literate consumer society was being used in management training, whereas managers were going to face situations in India where the economy was totally closed and business operated under a mass of government regulations. Marketing examples from textbooks had little application beyond the small confines of developed urban markets. In a practical sense, Indian management of that era needed primarily to learn how to cope with government restrictions, deal with bureaucrats, pre-empt other people's industrial licences, and substitute imports at all stages. They did not have to worry a great deal about costs or quality in a heavily protected market. All this would have been anathema to the writers of the textbooks that they were reading in their courses. It was fondly hoped that with the right minds, assessment and sifting of data and cross-fertilization with like-minded persons in a congenial ambience, the right response to changing situations would ultimately be produced, but nobody expected this to be achieved as a direct result of the training.

Even sophisticated quantitative techniques like operations research, accounting projections like the discounted cash flow and statistical quality control which were being competently taught in management institutes found little actual application in industry, to the frustration of the qualified entrant.

Our strength, in those days, was the exposure which practising managers had in the field of personnel management at large which management institutes could indigenize fairly quickly, although not till the eighties had the contents of that learning reached a level where the discipline could genuinely be called human resource development. This had, of course, already happened in the individual disciplines. At the beginning of the period and for quite some time after, large corporations would have chief accountants who were not qualified chartered accountants. The same organizations by the early sixties could not dream of employing a non-qualified accountant even in one of the branch accounts departments; personnel Managers were going through specialized training programmes to increase their competence; and production management had recently been included in the curriculum of engineering colleges.

A big problem lay in the area of appropriate incentives for managers. The cardinal incentive for managers abroad was distinctly materialistic—a salary structure which allowed accumulation of wealth and comfortable provisions for retirement, stock options, and a host of such facilities practically none of which was available to the Indian manager. His salary, meagre by any objective standard, was severely restricted and eroded by draconian taxation. Even as recently as the mid-eighties, the highest salary permissible to the Chairman of an Indian company was a ridiculous Rs 60,000 per year with a share in the profits of up to Rs 30,000. Perquisites to bolster his living standards created artificial priorities which could not be sustained in retirement, the very prospect of which caused deep depression and trauma, whereas his counterpart abroad greatly looked forward to the affluent days of freedom in retirement. Not unnaturally, where an opportunity existed many succumbed to corrupt means of increasing earnings—sometimes officially encouraged by the Board.

The scene changed rapidly from the eighties and today the Indian manager and director can, with a successful career spanning a lifetime, live in great comfort through his pension, honestly accumulated savings from a very handsome salary, and many other facilities. Monthly earnings in the range of Rs 3-5 lakhs for company heads whose predecessors only fifteen years ago drew Rs 5,000-10,000 are commonplace.

There was also an organizational problem. Western literature was based on companies which were truly owned by a wide-ranging number of shareholders. In India, barring a few exceptions, majority control was either in the hands of foreigners, an Indian business family, or a government department so that whilst a senior corporate manager could take a number of important decisions on operational issues, decisions on crucial matters concerning the company were not fundamentally taken by its own Board, that is by Indian professional managers, but by either foreign professionals,

Indian businessmen, or Indian bureaucrats or ministers.

Under the circumstances, the Indian manager of the time could continue to derive satisfaction and pleasure from his profession only if his driving motive was the challenge of the immediate job and a conviction that in his own way he was contributing to the economic development of the country. This may sound a bit pompous but this certainly was the predominant motivation of the sensitive and qualified manager. This reflected itself in the migration— often at great sacrifice of salary and, more particularly, of freedom with perquisites—to the public sector for a perceived greater managerial challenge and doing a job directly useful to the country. Indeed this was a big opportunity that public sector undertakings (PSUs) in a significant phase of their development squandered. If the PSU world at large could have seen the successful assimilation of such entrants more would have followed, and the quality of public sector results could have been different. This was, however, not to be because of the lack of perception in those who sat at the commanding heights of the economy, their desire to meddle and politicize purely business issues, and the petty jealousies of entrenched, not too competent, managers and bureaucrats in the public sector at the time.

The class which entered the managerial fold carried some of its background traits and lifestyle into its jobs which it took more than one generation of training and ruthless exposure to iron out. There was, for example, scant appreciation of the role of capital and in the way managerial duties were allocated this shortcoming was further heightened. Indian managers learnt very quickly the essence of management in production and became very good at reduction of operating costs in personnel, marketing, and even accounting (with the exception of finance, that is capital planning and management, which knowledge and exposure came much later). In managerial parlance, they could be said to have been excellent profit and loss account operators but poor in balance sheet. Business is ultimately balance sheet. This lacuna spilled over into their own personal lives as well, accentuated by low salaries, pretentious ways of living, and high taxation. There were few instances of professional managers of that era consciously building up capital. The lack of personal capital restricted their options in entrepreneurship; unlike today's crop they were destined to use all their experience and expertise to increase somebody else's wealth instead of having a crack at developing their own enterprises which some of them dearly wanted to do.

In 1974, at the height of government control over Indian industry and following the nationalization of major banks, the Government of India set up a committee under P.L. Tandon to devise norms for providing bank credit to industry. The Tandon formula that was evolved specified margins for a range of items including book debts and inventories. To many highly placed operating managers, this brought a revelation about the importance of capital. Hitherto, reduction of inventories or collection of debts had been seen more as an exercise in discipline rather than a direct contribution to the company's profits. Managers had operated on the basis of working hard to generate a good profit and loss statement. It was now brought home to them that what mattered more was the simple axiom that at the end of the day cash-in must exceed cash-out for the business to survive and grow and the velocity of capital turnover was more important than profit percentage on turnover. Instances were not rare where companies were showing healthy returns on turnover but were hopelessly cash-strapped with bloated slow-moving inventories and debtors' lists. What is more intriguing is that banks which had hitherto exercised discretion on the basis of their knowledge of their clients, began using the Tandon formula mechanically. The result was that an engineering company which had, up to then, been generally cash surplus and yet by every acceptable business norm genuinely needed to be supported with substantial credit facilities, was denied such credit purely because the average net current assets and inventories over the past three years could not support the Tandon formula for lending.

Societal values and the perquisite structure which put a high premium on the generalist discouraged the continuous development of functional specialization. If all the trappings of office indicated to the outside world that the General Manager of an organization in a region was apparently more successful than him, the specialist—say potentially the best operations research man in India—working with an organization chose to be General Manager at which he was perhaps a mediocrity, rather than be known as the best operations research expert in the country. The country, too, lost a much needed specialist. Happily organizations have recognized this fact and remuneration structures are beginning to be designed to stop such undesirable deviations in career paths.

Indeed, the perquisite structure, designed to help the executive round the stranglehold of taxation, produced warped values. There was a limit to the flat/house rent that could be paid to an executive linked to his salary; if the rent exceeded this limit, the extra was to be added to the executive's income for tax purposes. To get around this, ownership of executives' accommodation by the company helped—and so large amounts of capital much needed for business were diverted to real estate. Indeed, in 1979, a company in Calcutta advertised its need for a bungalow for its Chief Executive for which it was prepared to pay Rs 60 lakhs! Translated revenue outgoing this meant an interest of Rs 9 lakh a year—for a Chief Executive whose official cost to the company with all the trappings of office did not exceed Rs 2.5 lakh. The security cost and other establishment support expenses on a manager's residence paid by the company often exceeded by far the official earnings of the manager.

The ultimate ambition of a successful manager was, and continues to be, to make it to the Board of his company. There is an aura of Olympian heights associated with the Boards of Indian companies when seen from below but which comes as a kind of anti-climax to the new entrant. In effect, the most general outcome of elevation to the Board is public perception of the way the manager is valued within the organization rather than any increase in responsibilities or intrinsic worth of the manager. At the same time, of course, under Companies' Law, he comes within the ambit of a lot of legal provisions and any Director in India who acts in ignorance of them or, as happens more often, flouts them, runs grave risk of which there are abundant examples in India's corporate history in recent decades.

A Director in the Western world operates in a Board where it is rare to find an outside overall controlling interest. When he sits on a Board, therefore, he is part of the policy-framing operation of the company. In India, the position is different.

We like to believe that we have professionally managed organizations but we have them only at unit level in reality. Almost without exception large public corporations in both the public and private sectors are owned by a power group which dictates policies regarding major investments and top management succession. Decisions on these matters are taken in the power group away from the company—it could be a family, it could be an individual or two in a multi-national headquarters many thousands of miles away, or it could be a bureaucrat or politician. In none of these cases are the shots really being called by an *Indian professional manager*. If he is a manager at all he is likely to be a foreigner or essentially a capitalist.

A company Board in India hardly ever discusses any crucial issue with the knowledge that its own discussions on the subject would be final. It is not a deciding authority in any real sense on any issue which will have a radical effect on the future of the company. That decision power rests with the majority shareholder; the function of the company Board is to generate the formal request and have it legally endorsed. There are, of course, organizations in India which are ultimately run by salaried individuals who are truly professional managers and have no dynastic stakes themselves or a mandate from a majority-owning group. The tragedy is that generally the atmosphere even in such rare organizations is so pervaded by the rule and style of management of organizations in the country that those at the helm imbibe the same attitude and powers and others acquiesce easily to their exercising such omnipotent powers. In other words, there are very few exceptions to the general rule that the manager-turned-Director cannot make the transition from the role of manager to discuss as an equal when sitting around a Board table. This happens in Western countries but the pervading culture in India does not foster it.

The situation was, of course, absolutely ridiculous when Directors' remunerations were draconically fixed at very low levels by the Company Law Board. Today, at least in the established organizations, elevation to the Board means not just recognition through honour but a handsome increase in remuneration and perquisites.

Another characteristic of the Indian professional manager, happily beginning to weaken in the last decade or so, is obsessive interest with job and career to the exclusion of hobbies, connections, and interests not linked with work. This makes career success a matter of passion, and failure to succeed in the rat race causes deep trauma. Worse, when retirement comes, more than financial problems, which in new salary structures are no longer acute, the absence of useful means of spending time becomes a serious problem. Here again, his Western counterpart in general lives through his working career for the day when he can really enjoy the best years of his life unfettered by routine and pursuing life long interests in reading, gardening, golf, and travelling—to speak only of general pursuits. If you ask managers what they will do on retirement, a fair majority will say they are engaged in consultancy or an alternate part time or full time job.

The exhausting rat race to the top of the pyramid in which many more will fail than succeed, makes the manager overlook the joys of life. A decent earning from an early stage in life with comfortable living standards, the facility to travel a lot within the country and often abroad, sufficient free time to pursue subjects of personal interest, and the opportunity to meet a wide cross-section of people are opportunities few professions offer. For long the Indian manager did not appreciate these as important in themselves.

But the strongest charge that needs to be made against the Indian manager is his alienation, regrettably growing, from the rank and file of the country and, therefore, the workforce. Strangely, this is a factor which seems to be increasing as a limited intermingling of classes is taking place through educational institutions. This is so obviously a drawback that there is no need to dilate on it; unless it is corrected the entire economic and social development of the country will be affected. Every industrial nation has its trade union problems but ours are exacerbated by the complete separation of the managerial class from the common people, heading towards a situation —in T.S. Eliot's words—of two sets 'too strange to each other even for misunderstanding'. In sports, in markets, the divide between the two is widening all the time. Where forty years ago young managers played in their corporate teams along with workers, today's managers take to golf, tennis, and similar exclusive pursuits.

FIVE

The Public Sector

The management of the public sector in India has, for the last three decades, been the subject of much discussion covering a wide spectrum of opinions and angles. Here I will not concern myself with the correctness or otherwise of the political compulsions which are responsible for the strong presence of the public sector in Indian business. My concern is with the management of this sector in the fifty years under review.

The government was already in commerce and industry even at the time of Independence or shortly thereafter. The Imperial Bank had been taken over, Indian Railways—although admittedly not run through conventional corporate management—was in every way a professionally managed industry. The erstwhile feudatory states like Mysore and Travancore had their own state-run industries. The ordinance factories required managerial skills to run as efficiently as they did for two hundred years.

The general record of management in almost every such sphere was one of success. Yet, by the end of the sixties, the management of the public sector was being universally criticized. Caught between the demands of dispensing social benefits on the one hand and the need to make profits on the other, and being answerable to a group of legislators who did not have clear concepts in the matter, public sector management grappled ineffectually with finding the right path.

After the adoption of the Industrial Policy Resolution of 1948, which was enshrined for execution under the Industries (Development & Regulation) Act, in 1951, and further endorsed by the Resolution of 1956, it was the firm policy of the government that the 'commanding heights of the economy' would henceforth be taken care of by direct government investment and control, in order to ensure proper allocation of resources on an appropriate priority basis. Thus, in the fifties Hindustan Steel (HSL), the Fertiliser Corporation of India, the Food Corporation of India (FCI), Indian Oil Corporation (IOC), Bharat Heavy Electricals (BHEL), and the Heavy Engineering Corporation (HEC) came into being as completely new entities and existing companies were taken over for the same reason and grouped together as in the case of Indian Airlines.

In later years the management of these companies has come in for a great deal of criticism for inefficiency, lack of enterprise, and squandering of funds. What goes unrecognized today is the fact that with a handful of young, often inexperienced, recruits from the existing two steel plants of Tata and Indian Iron, which collectively produced at the time only 1.5 million tonnes of finished steel, HSL conceived, completed, and reached a production of nearly four million tonnes of steel within a decade, through three widely separated independent steel plants, two of them in back-of-

the beyond regions. At the same time, the entire concep-
tual framework of a four million tonne steel plant at Bokaro
was finalized. Contrast this with the time it has taken to
plan and put into execution, Visakhapatnam, and its cost
overruns after the country had been producing high- grade
technologists and trained professional managers by the hun-
dreds for three decades.

In the sixties, the craze for public sector industry was
such that small industries were being set up in this sector,
which could not be justified under the concept of the
'commanding heights'. Nor were these areas reserved for
the public sector. Thus, the government got into the
manufacture of bread, pesticides, plate vessels, and machine
tools, which the private sector, given the freedom, would
have found the capital to run successfully and competitively
as it was already doing in these fields.

In the seventies, the public sector arena got heavily
contaminated by the rampant taking over of sick companies.
Whatever the reason, in many individual companies the
fact of the matter was the company had run itself to the
ground and the management stood discredited. The total
score book of public sector management and statistics was
polluted by the heavy influx of such companies, adding fuel
to public wrath against the quality of management in the
public sector.

There were, at the same time, justifiable takeovers.
The Indian Copper Corporation was considered to have
inadequate resources for the potential development of the
company which the country needed to organize. Between
1970 and 1973, the nationalization of coal mines was
completed with the declared objective of mechanizing
coalmining, improving productivity through cross-holding

extractions and generally making it possible to invest heavily.

Yet another type of nationalization—for questionable objectives—was the creation of State Trading Corporations (STCs). They took advantage of the highly restricted Import Control Policy and set up government-supported import-canalizing agencies, giving them monopoly status, and promoted exports by spending export promotion funds which were denied to the private sector.

I have been describing the different types of public sector companies created at different stages, in order to make some observations on the quality of management in this sector. If one went to an HSL work-site in the fifties, one could not but have been impressed by the total dedication of management all along the line, specially at the middle or lower range, to the task at hand and the pride in the part it was playing in building up 'the temples of modern India', as Nehru so proudly called these ventures. Such commitment all along the line at Bokaro Second Stage or Visakhapatnam is conspicuously absent. Likewise, a visit to the dam sites under construction at DVC or Bhakra Nangal, was an uplifting experience because of the sheer enthusiasm of the team, which is totally missing at similar project sites today.

The fact of the matter patently is that somewhere down the line operational management has lost its satisfaction and pride in the job at hand. This has come about as a result of lack of leadership and inspiration from the top which, in turn, has been caused by political meddling, jobbery, and the planned diversion of the immense resources of such organizations for personal gains. The availability of alternative avenues of employment whereas one took jobs in the past with few options may also be a contributory factor.

From a management point of view, a very disconcerting feature of public sector organization was the absence of a policy of promotion to the top from within. Almost every public sector company in the sixties and seventies going into the eighties, had Chairmen who were not there by the natural process of promotion from within (with the sole exception of HSL). Public sector companies were generally great supporters of management education and spent enormous amounts on their executives' training both within the organization and outside but the fruits of this training were hardly ever reaped as over the years ennui settled upon the organization. A closed economy did not allow assessment of true competitiveness and it was more important to develop skills in preparing acceptable explanations for failure and answering parliamentary queries.

There were some peculiar attendant risks in public sector jobs. A coal mine manager in the private sector could move from one coal mine company to another developing his career. With the coalmining industry nationalized, one was necessarily stuck and if job satisfaction in a particular context did not arise, there was little chance of the affected manager seeking a change with the facility to use his specialization in a new environment of his choice. The same problem, to a large extent, confronted steel metallurgists.

It is also perhaps true that in those early years the young engineers, accountants, marketing and personnel people who came into the public sector through an objective selection process were gratified by the opportunity to undertake challenging jobs where for comparable jobs entry into the private sector was more influence based. As the years went on this was no longer a factor as qualified personnel by and large never failed to get an acceptable opening in either sector.

The Public Sector Enterprises Board (PSEB) set up to monitor and assess the progress of public sector companies and running them at the top, could not be expected to do more than continuously stamp out fires as they were cropping up everywhere. It would have been a much more effective policy to strengthen the Boards of individual companies with Directors, with the mandate and power to get results. All in all, an immense bureaucracy was created where the input–output ratio was abysmal. The number of major public sector organizations which were going headless for long periods due to delays in finding incumbents was almost scandalous.

Lack of adequate monetary incentive was often adduced to explain the weaknesses of public sector management. This was hardly true up to middle management level, where the differences in remuneration on a total package basis between the public and private sectors, were by no means significantly different. However, since the difference was noticeable at the top, the dissatisfaction of top management went right down the organization and affected executive productivity. What was necessary was to make effective comparison of the level and quantum of responsibility which a young man was carrying in these giant public sector organizations, in contrast to his counterpart in the private sector; positions should have been rationalized to increase responsibility and improve remunerations, instead of expanding numbers, reducing every time the individual slice. More than remuneration, recognition, accolades, and public appreciation were lacking whilst favouritism was rampant.

Notwithstanding the known shortcomings, hazards, and problems faced by public sector chiefs, instances were by no means unknown where a successful private sector executive was willing to changeover. Motivation in those cases was a mixture of various factors. The challenge of the public sector post by its sheer size and ramifications was attractive, whilst the relatively easy access to the top in his own private sector domain engirdled by restrictions on growth by government policy bred a sense of ennui. Heavy personal taxation played a part as well.

An amusing example, by no means fictitious, of a company Director may be cited. He had in 1972 a salary of Rs 7500 with numerous perquisites including free furnished accommodation for which 12.5 per cent was added on to his salary. His take home pay was Rs 2600. He was entitled to a commission on the profits of the company at 50 per cent of his annual salary. On the Rs 45,000 which this amounted to, the 12.5 per cent for accommodation had to be added and since he was already in the 93 per cent marginal rate bracket (over Rs 1 lakh per year) his total taxation on his commission amounted to Rs 46,506! Obviously he wanted to return the commission but was warned that since he had become entitled to it by shareholders' voting he may be liable to Gift Tax! He was prepared to face that risk!

Frankly, at the ministry level, there was scant appreciation of how industry operated. In the late fifties, when the Indian Oil Corporation (IOC) IOC was being developed, a young man of 26, working in a British-owned company as junior officer, drawing a salary of Rs 1300 per month, met the then

Petroleum Minister through family connections and asked whether he could not be considered for the then newly formed IOC. The Minister replied, as a friend of the family, he would advise the young man to wait till he was about 35, when his salary in the private sector could be expected to have crossed Rs 1000 because that would be an impressive point for being considered for the public sector. In later years, at 35, the person in question had joined the Board of his company which was ranked amongst India's top industry leaders.

A breath of fresh air in the government's perception of how industry should be run was introduced by Mohan Kumaramangalam, who from 1970 was Minister for Steel & Industry. He appreciated the need for freeing public sector industries from the shackles of government control and brought in the concept of a holding company like the Steel Authority of India Ltd (SAIL), which would allow a great deal of autonomy to government firms. He died in an air crash, unfortunately too soon after the creation of SAIL which rapidly lapsed into total bureaucratic control, thereby adding yet another layer of management control for public sector companies.

Kumaramangalam was also responsible for the nationalization of the coal industry and is accused for the failing of that industry today. He did not have an opportunity to put his ideas into operation and practice, and what he created turned to havoc through uncommitted managers widely accused of corruption.

Kumaramangalam came from a Communist background and it was his favourite saying to industry chiefs in his domain that because of his background he was constantly pressed to introduce workers' participation in management, but he steadfastly refused to consider this because the Indian public sector's prime need was to ensure the participation of managers in management. This was a pertinent observation but regrettably the lacuna persists.

Mohan Kumaramangalam had succeeded in attracting a number of talented persons to join public sector undertakings in his command area. Practically every one of them left the public sector before retirement as they faced conditions inimical to continuing after him.

In later years, the trend was in fact reversed when experienced public sector managers began being offered lucrative senior assignments in the private sector. This at least showed that rambling and unprofitable though they were, public sector undertakings had become part of the corporate management mainstream by virtue of their size and complexities.

There was also an element of pragmatic patriotism for some in the decision to move to the public sector. The country was manifestly heading towards socialistic control of industry and if one could not beat them one joined them if a good offer came one's way to head a major public sector unit.

However, to most of those who did make the transition, whilst job challenges remained satisfying, the continuous jealousy of the bureaucracy caused serious exasperation. The Joint Secretary in the concerned ministry had immense powers over an enterprise in his wing but resented the higher salary and apparently attractive perquisites the industrial manager enjoyed. The manager was not generally equipped with the savvy to handle political pressure to which he was relentlessly exposed both at plant site and at New Delhi. The looming threat of a CBI investigation soon forced him to become rulebound and, therefore, slow in decision making. Worst of all, he realized on the departure from the ministry of the person who had encouraged him to changeover, that contrary to general perception, public sector management was far more personality oriented than what prevailed in the private sector.

However difficult and unworkable the system might be, under the right leadership even that system can be incomparably successful. Although strictly not a public sector organization, but one deeply involved with politicians and local influences, is Kaira Co-operative (AMUL) whose spectacular success under V. Kurien is hailed the world over. In the early sixties, Hindustan Machine Tools (HMT), responding to the dynamism of Chairman Mathulla, embarked on a course of setting up a new plant every two to three years on its own cash generation. Twenty years after him, HMT is struggling to keep afloat.

In the case of smaller public sector companies, operating in fields where private sector competitors also featured, their slow decision making, high overheads on social amenities and labour welfare, and poor management, generally made them nonstarters. As for taken-over companies, subsequently nationalized, there is hardly any success story of figures or specific achievement. Cash support from the government and 10 per cent price premium on quotations to other public sector firms over private sector competitors were crutches which failed to prop the organizations up into self-sufficiency but rather encouraged perpetual dependence.

In, therefore, summing up the state of management in the public sector, if one has to generalize, one would say that the foundation was good and somehow the importance of the job in nation building seemed to have been transmitted down the line at first. It is also a general fact that where a management grows with an enterprise such management is able to adapt itself to the changing scale and nature of the enterprise. Where, however, an enterprise is born full grown, or managers from outside are inducted mass scale, an undue burden falls on the management and it is unable to cope with the problems that are inherent in such large and complex, or already very sick, organizations. However, with the general deterioration of political morals, ruthless closing of the economy killing any competitive edge, and the unfamiliarity of political bosses and meddling parliamentarians with what makes industry tick, the motivation seems to have evaporated. The opening of the floodgates of nationalization of sick industries gave public sector management as a whole, unwarrantedly, a bad name. The free access of trade union leaders to the controlling heights of the public sector did great harm to management morale on the ground. Otherwise the fundamental public sector companies like HSL, IOC, FCI, STC, BHEL were all getting excellent managerial input material, comparable with the best that the private sector got; their managers had jobs with tremendous responsibility which they were not given adequate authority to discharge. Individually they were all trained very well through professional management education inputs but the country failed to derive adequate return from the overall investment on them as a result of the huge hiatus between the shop-floor and ultimate decision-making authorities.

The inbuilt frustration of public sector management set it on the path of confrontation. A special feature in the world of Indian management was the growth of officers' associations which operated virtually as trade unions.

Collective representation of executives was not a unique feature—banks in this country as well as abroad have strong officers' associations; so do government employees although not as effectively. In both these cases, however, there has always been a large identity of interests and issues were confined to specifics. In bringing under one umbrella many different kinds of organizations and, therefore, issues, such associations lost their focus; engendered deeper frustration, and lost the sympathy of the public at large.

SIX

Changing Profiles

F rom the immediate post-War manager of questionable sophistication in the modern professional context to the bright young bushy-tailed MBAs matching the brightest in the world at the end of this century, the Indian manager has undergone continuous evolution. To understand Indian management of the last fifty years, it would be necessary and interesting to study that changing profile. Obviously the discussion is on the trend of the largest numbers and ought not to be disproved by pointing out exceptions.

MANAGING AGENCIES

The start must be made with the managing agency system. Some comment about its history has already been made in Chapter 1. If one leaves out the burgeoning technocrats in the textile mills and coalmines, management *qua* management was predominantly in the fold of the managing agencies, both British and Indian. At the end of the Second World

War, managing agencies were at the height of their influence. Each commanded a vast variety of industrial and trading activity—jute, textiles, plantations, mines, shipping, insurance,—to mention only the common items. Several had major engineering concerns—mechanical, chemical, and electrical—under their wings; some managed electricity supply companies; Tata Sons and Martin Burn—both Indian owned—were managing agents for two integrated steel plants with their own coal and iron ore mines. These were essentially run by executives situated at the head office in metropolitan cities. Even for Tata Iron & Steel the major decisions were made by the managing agents. Each executive would have several wide-ranging or a variety of companies under his control; he would be moved from one group to another. It was not believed that there was any need for him to have a detailed familiarity with the processes of the managed company. Their management consisted essentially of organizing finance, placing key personnel, and overseeing purchases and sales. For most, except the Directors or partners, this was essentially a staff job. It was quite common, for example, for the juniormost executive in the plantation division of a managing agency head office or tea gardens division, to deal with seniormost members of broker firms and administer discipline to an errant plantation manager many years and many rupees his senior. The agency office was held in great awe in the managed units.

There could be a great deal of difference in the responsibilities carried by these executives and their management's perception of such responsibilities. For example, a person of the 'covenanted' cadre could purely be handling cash vouchers and office transport whilst another procured supplies against a managed engineering firm's indents—jobs which in the emerging industrial organizations were probably being done by non-executive staff. By and large, it would be fair to state that up to the middle management level at least, executives in Indian-owned managing agencies carried a far heavier work load and had greater responsibilities than their counterparts in British-owned firms. Their frustration, as earlier stated, was at not being able to reach the top and feeling, on the whole, underpaid in relation to their counterparts in foreign-owned agencies.

The need for such jobs in a managing agency dictated the recruitment of persons who were able to hold their own politely in arguments, but be submissive to the discipline of agency bosses; as far as purchases went, most agencies had long-established supplier families—supplying everything from pins to motorboats—and the executive was supposed to deal firmly and politely with such a supplier; quality of correspondence in English was important. Again, in the Indian-owned agencies, suppliers and dealers were generally chosen on the basis of their acceptability to the owner's family (and could, in several instances, be run by offshoots of such families). Honesty and transparency were important. Familiarity with the staff was vetoed in British firms and more than one case can be recalled where a young probationer lost his job for speaking to the clerks in Bengali in separate managing agencies. The generic term 'babu' covered every staff member who was not covenanted. In later years a kind of junior management cadre euphemistically termed 'local management cadre' came into being as opposed to the covenanted which was the 'overseas management cadre' with contracts vetted by the home office. Able, educated personnel joined this group and the company could have effected a major saving in operating expenses, but there seems to have been little planning of a different way of sharing the work load. Promotions from the 'local' to the 'overseas' cadre were also few and far between, but *babus* had opportunities to go into the junior management group which they welcomed. However, caste distinction between covenanted and non-covenanted remained in lunch facilities, seating arrangement, toilets, and many small issues. In Indian-owned managing agencies, at least, the division was largely between owners and very senior managers and a broad spectrum of other executives. No great intellectual calibre was demanded or even preferred. 'Backgrounds' by and large determined the suitability of a person for the job.

In most of the companies managed by an agency, the agents had a controlling block of shares. The ownership of the agency was, therefore, in most cases an advertisement for the successful running of the managed companies which were in any case tied down with multi-faceted agreements with the agency. However, after Independence, whilst a section of British agencies wanted to hold on they found it difficult to raise funds for the expansion and modernization of some of the managed units without bringing in a lot of their own capital from abroad. Individual shareholders in India and the UK began to sell their shares in nervousness. What began with a selective sale of some of the companies—jute mills and tea gardens mainly—ultimately led to the sale of the agencies themselves when imports began to be severely restricted. In two cases—Balmer Lawrie and Andrew Yule—the Government of India stepped in to buy the controlling shares.

By the fifties the managing agency system had, of course, long been under review by the government but there were reservations about disturbing something that seemed to be working satisfactorily. The 1956 amendment of the Companies Act virtually brought the managing agency system in its own name to an end, although the practice effectively continued through managing agencies calling themselves secretaries of the managed companies. In 1970, however, the system was totally abolished.

There was adequate notice, therefore, of the impending demise of the system but astonishingly the managerial personnel did not see the writing on the wall and equip themselves for alternative arenas of employment. With Independence, a number of new industries were coming into India, with direct foreign investment or in collaboration with Indian partners. Very rarely did they place themselves under the umbrella of a managing agency but set up self-contained organizations of their own and raised minority equity in the share market after establishing the operation. The hardboiled managing agency executives had compared themselves with ICS officers. However, the difference was that whichever job the ICS officer took on, his experience was hands on. He could, therefore, one day be a District Magistrate, in his next posting be Chairman of a port, and move on again to be Textile Commissioner. His training, intellectual capability, and deep involvement with the job at hand soon earned him respect for his knowledge of the job itself and his style of operation. He was also assisted by a senior body of permanent staff in each posting which was knowledgeable in the area over which he had come to preside. No counterpart of that system existed in managing agencies. There were clerks, section heads, and executives who knew the paperwork and the routine but not the processes of the managed company.

In 1973, three years after the demise of the managing agency the head office staff of a major unit of the erstwhile agency was drawn from the old agency. Each department wrote to another in formal terms signing 'For the Company': the managed unit was dealing with its own head office as if it was a separate company!

The sons of families which controlled managing agencies, that is Indian-owned agencies, did not suffer from this limitation. Their early training was almost invariably in one or many of the production units on a hands-on basis, whereas in British companies the posting was almost entirely at the headquarters. The knowledge of the key personnel and key performance areas of the managed companies of Indian agencies was, therefore, sound.

The essential purpose of the 1956 Act was an attempt to improve the quality of corporate management by making it responsive to shareholders, providing a built-in mechanism through the widest possible disclosure of the company's working and financial position as well as providing not only judicial remedy but also direct government control over a large area of corporate management functioning. The objective of these regulatory measures was to impose a degree of discipline on corporate management so as to ensure clean administration for the benefit of shareholders and the community. They also aimed at providing a code of conduct under which an enlightened top management could achieve the highest standard of performance, measurable by generally accepted yardsticks of input and output. Introducing the 1956 Act, the precise words of C.D. Deshmukh, then Finance Minister, were: 'The managing agency system at a future date—not at a very distant future—will be abolished but the time, pace and the manner of its abolition are left to the Government.'

What is amazing is that even with such a clear warning, managing agencies continued to recruit and breed superficial managers. The new industrial companies were taking on young graduates and subjecting them to intensive factory training at salaries much less than agencies still gave their young executives. However, when these young men in industries were put on the job, from the firm's point of view, their approach was holistic and their involvement with the job and, therefore, the company was considerable; and their job satisfaction outweighed remuneration disparities.

In the seventies when the managing agency system came to a grinding halt, and the remnants were bought over by Indian trading houses, the job market was flooded with pathetic executives past their thirties, too old and too ill-equipped to find gainful employment in the industrial firms that were rising all over India. Had there been a sensible view of the future and training and job experience suitably tailored, a modernized managing agency system would have made a worthwhile contribution to the continuous growth of Indian management by pooling the talent of managers.

THE OIL COMPANIES

Next to the managing agencies, in size, spread, and extent of employment of management personnel, at the beginning of the period came the oil companies—Burmah Shell and Standard Vacuum (later Esso) were the two great giants whilst Caltex trailed somewhat behind and Indo-Burma Petroleum was a distant fourth. Even before Independence, Burmah Shell had opened the doors of the senior management cadre to Indian youth, quite often of Oxbridge extraction. Standard Vacuum and Caltex's management policies showed, in contrast, American influence. Direct recruitment into senior cadres was not open to Indians for quite a while. They had to work their way up from relatively lower rungs. However, by the fifties they were also recruiting young Indian men directly into their higher levels.

Burmah Shell's presence in India was ubiquitous. Its marketing network fanned out into remote corners of the country and a hierarchical control organization from district level through regional headquarters to the India head office was similar to the country's administrative set-up. Managers were posted in the districts and the job involved constant touring and dealing with distributors who were not sophisticated like them. This played a valuable part in their character build-up. Like the government, the oil companies did not allow executives to be posted too long in the same district—largely to avoid unsavoury relationships being forged. Although the job had no competitive edge, the exposure to the country was valuable and in later years when the foreign control over oil companies was dismantled, the executives quitting, by and large, found reasonable placements.

With the creation of the Indian Oil Corporation in the mid-fifties and gauging the mood in developing countries the oil companies engaged in a massive public relations campaign to secure people's support for their continuance, thereby influencing government policy. The public relations department was raised to a very serious level hardly matched since then and executives had massive inputs in this art. It was a losing battle and by the seventies the foreign oil companies had all departed. However, the organisations they built up carried on effectively, the hierarchical distance between the management and staff being filled with a number of intermediate positions.

NATIONAL MARKETING

Somewhat akin to the management structure, geographical reach, and the emphasis on both public relations as well as consumer advertising of the oil companies was the case of the Imperial Tobacco Company (today ITC Ltd.). Sophisticated executives were rotated in district postings and taught to sit cross-legged with dealers and owners of outlets selling cigarettes. A responsive top management and intensive and continuous internal training facilities overcame any doubts that might have arisen in the executives' minds about the net utility of making a career out of encouraging people to smoke. The management turnover was very small indeed and the company adroitly handled government relations and staved off nationalization.

The other marketing giants like Lever Brothers (today Hindustan Lever) and Bata pooled their management talent in regional headquarters and dealt through a wide network of dealers or outlet shops. Others, notably toiletries and pharmaceutical manufacturers, relied on distributing agents like Parry & Co, Geoffrey Manners, Muller & Phipps, TTK and Sons, to name a few, who in turn provided useful variety to the training of marketing personnel. It is difficult to appreciate today that as recently as the sixties Britannia biscuits, Pond's talcum powder, leading brands of toothpaste, or popular medicines were in fact reaching consumers through selling agencies appointed by the manufacturers.

Gradually, as the volume of business grew, the companies began operating their own marketing set-ups and the importance of the selling agencies dwindled. However, through the sixties all these organizations had played a valuable part in developing techniques of marketing as opposed to selling.

INDEPENDENT MANAGED INDUSTRIES

The emphasis shifted through the sixties to management in the companies which ran their own affairs through their own Boards. British firms soon realized that the market could not readily give them suitably trained managers and most of the enlightened organizations launched on the management trainee system in which they had just begun to invest in their own country. In the first place these companies had scant tradition or culture of their own and by and large their staff and directors were unfamiliar with the management trainee concept at work. Different types of treatment were accorded to management trainees—from established executive status to the midshipman concept—but all slogged hard at their training, often inviting the raillery of their pampered friends in agency houses. However, by and large, in learning the job thoroughly hands on, these early management trainees developed a strong rapport with the men they were later to command. What is more important, the success of the scheme established management trainees as a class in the best organized firms. As all this was happening in an era when job-hopping was rare and frowned at, the loyalties generated were strong. Today, we have sophisticated young men joining organizations as trainees or, more precisely, crown princes, at fabulous starting salaries. They do not find it necessary to learn the fundamentals of the company's business and use their training period to improve their own marketability.

In most of these industrial companies, career promotion was rapid as a recruit got in at the bottom level of management and rose with the successes of the company. Through the fifties and sixties, through import substitution, market gapfilling, and the general expansion of the economy, most

companies were on a trail of successes only to be jarred by
the Plan holiday period and consequent recession of three
years from 1966–9. By then the first generation had made
their mark and their entrance into Boardrooms in the late
thirties was becoming a common feature.

Salaries and perquisites in these companies were well
below agency levels and the Directors tended to compare
their Indian staff with the salary level of the old established
Indian industries. However, as the Indian recruits began
proving their worth and chafed at the discrimination *vis-a-
vis* expatriate staff, the Boards began to appreciate the fact
that there should be the same pay for the same job and it
would be a wise policy to raise Indian salaries and reduce
expatriate numbers. In any event, the foreign executives left
in large numbers after the massive devaluation of the Indian
rupee in 1966. By then Indian professional management
was in place and no MNC operation suffered as a result.

MULTI-NATIONAL COMPANIES

Whatever the political posturing at different times and from
different platforms may be, there can be no denying the
fact that MNCs have played a very big part in the fashion-
ing of Indian managers. That they were motivated by
profit-seeking can hardly be held against them; but in the
process they helped to accelerate the pace of induction and
training of first class Indian managers.

Technology is something India could at some financial
and time cost have acquired on her own; but the contribution
of MNCs to the concept of modern marketing requires
special mention.

Obviously a diverse group like the MNCs had varying

characteristics. Some could with justification have been accused of racial discrimination. But those who stayed and prospered fairly early after Independence began to see their Indian managers as, in every way, the equal of their own nationals. From the seventies started the healthy practice of Indians being posted abroad—not as learners but in top management positions. Soon they were attaining Board positions in the more enlightened and truly global companies of which Unilever remains a shining example.

At the end of the half century the time had come for companies in India themselves to move towards becoming MNC headquarters. This is the prospect and challenge of the second half century.

THE ERA OF SPECIALISTS

As these industrial companies grew and began running into adverse weather at times the need for specialists began to be felt, in the more sophisticated organizations at first and then as general practice. This was accentuated by a similar change that had taken place in the parent companies abroad and, of course, by the growing complexities of modern business. Hence accountants had to have strong professional education to get into any decent organization; yet right into the fifties, a company as successful and professional as Imperial Tobacco, preferred to take raw graduates and teach them the 'Imperial Tobacco way of accounting'. Personnel management was beginning to use jargon which necessitated formal training to acquire specialist status. New disciplines like operations research, statistical quality control, work study/industrial engineering were finding jobs for highly trained specialists. Advanced marketing companies were beginning to use market research and business economics.

However, as noted in an earlier chapter, the social culture of the time choked the development of specialists who vied for the generalist slots in top management. India soon started breeding a new category of qualified senior managers who could best be described as 'specialized generalists'.

It is no coincidence that in a large number of cases, the first Indian CEO of an MNC's Indian branch was an accountant. Global headquarters felt more secure entrusting their Indian companies to a professional, who spoke a common business language and would *per se* be a party to any attempt to maximize profits. The success of these appointees also proved how specialists could switch to the highest echelons of general management.

PUBLIC RELATIONS

A constant concern from the end fifties when the government's tentacles started gripping industry hard was about the 'image of the company'. As it became clear that under the Industrial Development & Regulations Act of 1951 it was extremely important to have a good image in the eyes of the government in order to get new industrial licences, expand, or install additional capacity, there was an obsession with public relations. Foreign companies almost seemed to have a sense of guilt in the face of continuous provocation from Indian-owned business and the ire of parliamentarians. Many felt threatened by impending nationalization. Most launched very expensive public relations campaigns. Every executive in the corporate house at that time was required to ensure not only that he did nothing to damage the company's image but also that he took every opportunity to project the company on suitable platforms. This was marked by liberal expenses on supporting executives' presence in Rotary and Lions Clubs, in prominent social clubs in the cities, and the holding of in-company and cross-company seminars to explain the importance of public relations. A common definition of Public relations is '90 per cent doing good and 10 per cent talking about it'; but only in rare cases did this proportion hold true.

The most glaring example of ultimately futile public relations was the back-to-the-wall battle of the oil companies to stave off nationalization. There was hardly a day in the late fifties and sixties when a newspaper in India did not carry the 'Burmah-Shell in India's Life and Part of It' campaign; the other major oil companies also had high-powered public relations departments that were empowered to monitor the actions of marketing personnel. However, as history has shown, this did not save these companies from nationalization and the general public does not appear to have shed too many tears.

Institutionalized public relations did not take root within company structure. One testimony is the fact that as far as I know, no fulltime public relations officer/specialist ever made it to the Board of any major company in India, although there was a long period of nearly two decades when every such company stressed the importance of institutionalized public relations and employed expensive personnel and gave them empires of their own.

LIAISON WITH GOVERNMENT

The Government of India's stranglehold on industry created from the end fifties a new specialization in top management—high powered executives to manage government relations in New Delhi. Expensive "embassies" were opened in the capital. The 'ambassador' necessarily had to be a very senior person who could deal without equivocation with top bureaucrats and ministers and who enjoyed the complete confidence of the company's chief executive who could be in Calcutta, Bombay, or Madras. No executive with age on his side and doing well in the mainstream could be expected to take up this assignment, however grand the trappings of office and fabulous the entertainment budget. Senior trusted personnel who had missed reaching the top of the ladder usually filled these posts; otherwise, an erstwhile government bureaucrat was recruited. To deal with government personnel at all levels, such 'ambassadors' had to create a parallel hierarchy in their own offices. A new specialization and an added layer of bureaucracy entered the private sector. Even public sector companies found it necessary to maintain such legations in New Delhi.

In course of time, many organizations found that the balance of the demand on the chief executive's time was such that the corporate planning office could, with benefit, move to the capital. In those cases, the need for a senior person specifically to deal with the government got minimized and this activity became merged with other corporate functions.

THE AGE OF MBAs AND INFORMATION TECHNOLOGY

By the eighties, the subsidiary floors of the corporate edifice were beginning to be heavily occupied by MBAs. That qualification seemed to have become the basic need for primary selection much as graduation used to be in a previous era.

With the base now so intellectually strong, India was finally ready, with a gap of not more than perhaps five years, for the era of information technology, to catch up with the developed world. This overlapped with the liberalization of economic policies and the entry into India of world-renowned financial consultancies. We now have a breed of managers who are basically fund managers and who get their first employments in their mid-twenties—usually through campus interviews—highly qualified and drawing salaries which, even allowing for inflation, are well beyond what Chairmen of companies used to get only ten years ago. They play for high stakes and accept the contingency of redundancy in the light of the company's fortunes. Very few have any intentions of sticking with the same company too long; in fact, very few wish to serve others any longer than they need to.

What has not yet been worked out is how such executives can lead men who are not as fortunately equipped as they are, to serve their organizations loyally.

WOMEN IN MANAGEMENT

No discussion of the changing profile can be complete without commenting on the entry of Indian women into management. Women from capitalist families had for some time been known to be associated with their family concerns but the entry of women as equal competitors to men in all branches of management actually commenced from the sixties. This process has gained enormous momentum in the last quarter of this century, so that more than a quarter of all students in institutions training for the MBA are women.

In advertising and tourism women have reached the top but their presence in the major Boardrooms of other industries in India is still very scant, to say the least. The reason should not be sought solely in male chauvinism, although it doubtless plays a part. To find a parallel one should go back to the development of MBAs themselves. At a time when it was commonplace in Indian firms— particularly MNC controlled ones—to find men entering the Boardroom at below 40, even twenty-five years after the first MBA came out, very few major companies had MBAs on their Boards although these companies had all recruited MBAs as trainees. There was a certain tendency towards job migration or entrepreneurship where funds permitted; staying power was suspect. Assumed discrimination often hastened departure before conditions ripened for rewards. Perhaps this is also true of woman executives, their problem exacerbated by marriage which does not really have a direct effect on men. Middle management in the corporate sector is bulging with women, trained, competent, and point for point as good as men; but the path to the top remains slippery for them.

Special mention need be made of the entry of women from entrepreneurial families into management. By and large, women from successful capitalist families have tended to launch out into their own manageable-sized enterprises like fashion boutiques, eateries, catering, and software. However, they are increasingly moving into the mainstream business of the family, especially where male siblings are absent. So far, unlike such male siblings they have tended to come in directly at the top rather than work their way up through the departments of the empire; nevertheless they are providing effective direction in their managed areas.

As compared to males there are still few women from such families who go to pre-experience management schools, but it is an increasing trend. The extent of the presence of women in the management of owner-managers' enterprises is comparable to similar organizational structures in the Western world or East Asia.

It is to be hoped that their successes will remove gender biases in commerce and industry in a wider sense. There already exist examples of women holding senior management positions in practically every sector from steel to banking but as yet their numbers are fewer than what a logical percentage should have shown.

SEVEN

Some Specific Areas

Discussion of management in the corporate sector tends to focus industrial companies and large conglomerates. No history of management can be complete without looking at some specific areas where the nature of the duty and the environment create specialized demands—which, however, fall within the ambit of management in every sense of the word. Here I will consider a few areas which have traditionally been employers of large numbers of managerial personnel as well as those new sunrise professions which attract competent managers abundantly. The list is by no means exhaustive but gives a fair idea of the wide variances in the development and lifestyles of different types of Indian managers during the period under review.

PLANTATION INDUSTRIES

Here I am essentially talking of the tea industry. Plantations in India include coffee, rubber, and spices but the running of these plantations other than tea is, with very few exceptions, essentially in the hands of the family members of the owners. Where they are not, the comparison with tea is close.

Tea industry management certainly in the modern age has suffered from a great deal of disinformation—partly because of an unsavoury history and partly because the tea planter has no presence in the normal fora of Indian management at large. To the uninitiated the image of a plantation manager suffers from a hangover of impressions created through literature concerning indigo planters in the last century and Mulk Raj Anand's *Two Leaves and a Bud* in the first half of this century. The general picture of the plantation manager in such quarters is of a grossly overpaid person, not particularly educated and a hard drinker. This is quite different from the rank of managers one would have been meeting for, at least, the last quarter of a century. What is also conveniently overlooked is that for two decades from 1950 there was hardly any movement in tea prices while costs went up inexorably, especially after 1957. Very few gardens went to the wall and this would not have been possible without plantation management playing its part fully.

A typical tea plantation organization would consist of a manager who is assisted by two assistant managers—one for the garden and the other for the factory. This has traditionally been and continues to be the structure. There is nothing at the next level above clerks. The three of them, living on a 500-800 hectare property with poor telecommunications, their bungalows kilometres apart, and more often than not bad connecting roads, are responsible for anywhere between 800–1500 workers—not just for their productive output but also for the accommodation of the family to rigid standards laid down, creches for babies, schools for children, supply of rations, full medical facilities for families, including a well-equipped and well-staffed hospital—all this subject to constant inspection by state authorities. In terms of added value, the output of an average estate could be in the region of Rs 3–6 crore. Imagine what a factory producing that much of added value and managing so many men with a mini–township, would have set up for the management structure. The unit manager would almost certainly have been supported by a personnel manager, a production manager, a commercial manager, and an accountant, some of whom in turn would have had some executive staff reporting to them.

The plantation manager reports to a group manager or visiting agent who may be in the district or located at the group head office far away. The industry developed a unique and effective system of ensuring conformity in labour practices and connected matters by membership of trade associations—The Indian Tea Association (ITA), Tea Association of India (TAI), United Planters Association of South India (UPASI)—which provide full personnel advisory services through their men located in each tea-growing district. Periodic wage negotiations are done on region- / industrywise basis with the operating unions and unit managers are freed from any involvement by the Associations' advisors and the elected committee members. The uniformity of wages and basic working conditions is exemplary in each region as is conformity. However, this in no way diminishes the responsibility of the plantation executive towards personnel administration, although legal aspects are fully taken care of by the advisor. The manager still remains responsible for discipline, law and order, and the general well-being of his personnel within broad guidelines monitored by the Association's advisor and government regulations. There is healthy camaraderie amongst planters of different companies in each tea district through a series of formal meetings—on all subjects ranging from labour to technical aspects, informal discussions, and club nights. This system, which has operated from before the beginning of the period under review, still persists, although with greatly improved communication by air and telecommunications the manager is very closely controlled from his group headquarters. This is in some ways a pity and tends to diminish initiative. After all, Britain began losing its Indian empire when the cable line from Whitehall to the Viceroy's office was connected and statesmen not conversant with conditions on the ground could dictate decisions.

At the beginning of the period, except for Indian-owned gardens, tea plantation management was almost exclusively British. First generation Indian managers were chosen for their health, gregariousness, and sporting abilities. Sons of families with tradition in land management, for example the Thakores of Rajasthan, were favoured. Over the years the educational qualification of the manager has risen greatly. In the past managing agencies looked after gardens on behalf of owners and the control system was one of revenue administration with the individual manager left largely on his own for the productive health of the estate. In this, the Tea Research Association based at Jorhat and funded partly by the Council of Scientific and Industrial Research and partly by industry, has done sterling work, particularly in respect of productivity in the tea garden as opposed to the tea processing factory. From instinctive experience-based reactions in the past, today's manager looks at drainage, selection of clones, and deployment of pesticides and fertilizers with a scientific eye. Largely due to a traditional hostility to inducting qualified engineers in the plantation's tea processing factories, a corresponding upgrading on the machinery side was delayed. Control from Britain through the India-based managing agency has now been replaced by direct control from a nearby headquarters and is far more intensive. The advantage now is that the entire decision-making chain is a connection of educated, knowledgeable persons with similar experiential backgrounds and fully *au fait* with contemporary problems on the ground. To turn now to the flip side of plantation managers. Their salary structure in the past was governed by consideration of isolation: a recognition providing for a high level of *mofussil* comforts to compensate the member's family for living in the wilderness and enable them to send their children to boarding schools. Today's plantations by and large are no longer isolated. The arterial roads are good, there are other factories and business establishments in the area, and in the north-east the presence of major Defence establishments and oil installations. Dish television has now reached most planters' homes. However, no changes have been made in the perquisites traditionally given. The official ITA standard for domestic servants on the company's roll for a manager's bungalow is still nine, and for the assistant manager, five. Just to show how immutable these conditions are, of the nine in the manager's bungalow, two were originally *bhistis* (water carriers). Today no manager's bungalow is without piped water supply, but the two report for duty! Traditionally, management in the plantation areas has tended to remain in tight islands of their own with scant regard for the environment or even welfare and development of their workers and their workers' children beyond what is demanded by legislation. The old British planters who did not go home for three to four years at a stretch and were hardly ever transferred from one garden to another developed, in many cases, a lot of interest in the countryside. Today's managers are frequently shifted from one garden to another and at the slightest opportunity they and their families go back to their home towns. As a result of acquisition of a lot of foreign-owned gardens by Indian businessmen and also as a result of political pressure, locals from the immediate area are getting into management staff. They spend their leisure hours away from the garden with relatives and friends in the area rather than strengthening the camaraderie centred around the area club which was a strong point of plantation life.

The net result of all this is that plantation managers continue to acquire job experience which, though very considerable in its own scope, is not marketable outside. Nor are they at home in all-India management circles along with representatives of other industries. If, therefore, a plantation manager has to quit the trade in his mid-thirties or later, his employability is poor and the avenue most accessible is trading in products and services used by the industry. A new area has opened up for some recently with the development of tea gardens in countries like Vietnam, Mauritius, and Malawi, which has created fair demand for the experienced Indian planter as consultant.

ADVERTISING

Right up to the advent of the seventies, when India operated a tightly closed economy and product competition was restricted, television had not penetrated Indian homes and advertising industry was a smalltime affair. The emphasis was on institutional advertising for public relations rather than brands. A few exceptions like toothpaste and cosmetic manufacturers had need for massive competitive advertising.

Consequently, those who went into the business were essentially attracted by the creativity and in many cases influenced by the status of the advertising industry in the developed countries. Salary structures were pitiable compared to established trading and industrial concerns and the prospects of promotion were limited. The most gainful outlet was to move from an agency to a large advertiser's firm.

Through the fifties and sixties there was, in fact, serious curtailment of advertising expenditure, when niggardly limits were put for tax exemption purposes. Leading agencies closed down or cut their operations and the picture was very bleak for the practitioner.

Starting from the mid-seventies there has come about a sea change. Now, in a liberalized economy, brand advertising is rampant. Since agencies cannot handle competitive products, more and more new agencies have come up well-supported with finance and clients from the beginning. The advent of television has given a scope which could hardly have been dreamt of. Computers, multi-media facilities, videos, and a host of other modern techniques have made sophisticated the tools of industry.

Today, the industry is one of the best paying for different levels of executives amongst all industries in India and is a great attraction for young people. The fast-paced, up-market lifestyle of the young executive from creativity to accounts handling is a constant attraction for bright young persons when academic excellence or MBAs are not mandatory for recruitment. Most leading advertising agencies have developed global links which give a wide perspective to young personnel. In every way, the advertising industry has emerged from the shadows on the Indian employment scene. The shackles of tax limits for exemption have been totally removed from advertising in recent budgets. Advertising in export markets, given a new flavour and corporate sponsorship of televised sports, presents exciting opportunities. At the same time, because of the high expenditure patterns now set in agencies they are less resilient in handling periods of downturns in business.

However, managers in the advertising business have come to be regarded as specialized personnel. Their career paths must, almost always, lie along advertising—not even marketing. Shifts in employment can only come by moving from agency to advertisers' companies to look after corporate publicity. Possibly in time lateral movement in those companies will set these executives on newer courses.

HOTEL AND TOURISM

Here again a completely new area of opportunities has come up in the last quarter of a century. Hotel or catering management is now a highly professionalized industry with reruitment almost exclusively from specialized training establishments. Tourism is not similarly equipped for pre- experience training but increasingly the success of established tourism organizations and the glamour of an international ambience, is attracting efficient young personnel who might have had prospects in other areas as well. Thus the image of a travel agency—an entrepreneur using a lot of low-paid men and women—has changed. All over India part-time courses—some very good—are available for the better training of tourism personnel. Indian tourism skill has to make quantum leaps, but at least the flow of suitable personnel can be arranged.

RURAL MANAGEMENT

A new avenue has developed since the eighties for professionalizing the management of industries in the rural sector such as dairies and agro-based industries. The creation of the Institute of Rural Management at Anand under Dr V. Kurien has opened up new vistas. As yet, this has to have wider acceptance in the choice of careers by young persons, but it is an interesting beginning. The graduates of the Institute find employment in the cooperative and corporate sectors and are wellequipped to turn entrepreneurs on their own in view of the considerable amounts of incentives that exist from funding sources.

SYSTEMS MANAGEMENT

Though not strictly in the corporate sector yet, organized management training leading to specialized MBA degrees is now being provided in several institutes for the professional management of hospitals, transport, energy, and the environment. With the number of large, sophisticated private sector hospitals and medical diagnostic centres that have been established and are coming up everywhere, professional management of hospitals will soon be widely in demand.

Likewise, transport has so far operated under an owner's close control but expansion of the trade and the availability of trained personnel will, by itself, generate new career opportunity especially since modern tools and techniques are widely known to augment productivity. In a country which has over a century trained and utilized one of the world's most efficient body of professional transport operators through the railway system, management of other forms of transport should become an important career opportunity if similar training inputs are provided and the industry presents the picture of an organized entity. Expansion of private airlines will also provide new opportunities. Coastal shipping and international shipping could also do with professional management to improve productivity and scope.

CONSULTANCY SERVICES

This is the latest boom occupation as far as the country's most talented young entrants are concerned. Since 1991 almost all leading American and European consultancy organizations have opened up operations in India and their campus recruitments from the leading management institutes outstrip salary offers from any other sector by far. The fact that the seniormost decision maker at the global head-quarters of Mckinsey, is a young Indian that almost every major worldwide consultancy company has an Indian partner, and that British and American management schools invariably have valued Indian personnel in their senior teaching staff give Indian managers prestige in this pursuit. The occupation is extremely demanding and whilst earnings are very high, the risks are correspondingly great. This is appreciated and does not seem to bother a generation whose parents had considered security of employment a matter of prime importance, while their starting salaries far exceed their parents' terminal earnings, even allowing for inflation.

The sophistication of the new young management consultants and financial consultants is truly impressive and they are global players in every sense of the word without having necessarily worked or even travelled abroad.

A special word needs to be said about financial consultancy services. Non-banking finance companies sprouted all over the country and were beginning to employ specialized managers. In the nineties most have been driven to the wall and there is little attraction now for young managers who had looked at this as an interesting career. However, the experience gathered has been put to use by the enterprising, to act as consultants for servicing and deploying finance.

SERVICES SECTOR

There is, of course, a vast and varied area of services which even two decades ago were run by owners through dedicated, ill-paid, unsophisticated personnel. In the last two decades these avenues are increasingly being taken note of by prospective entrants. Their operations have been modernized with the help of computers; many of them were started by foreign companies coming to India. One would mention in this category freight forwarding, retail sales management, warehousing, publishing—to name just a few. All of them are now benefited and made more interesting by the use of computers with exciting software and advanced telecommunication facilities which is the basis for professionalization.

Take for instance the case of a service industry like freight forwarding. It is not an area which has traditionally attracted or even today attracts bright young entrants—MBAs from premier institutions. In the eyes of the lay public it is equated with the kind of service which a packer and mover may offer on transfer of residence. Yet today global cargo movement is an industry vital in the sphere of international trade and its effectiveness has been immeasurably enhanced by advancement in electronics—in data processing and telecommunication where large sums are spent. To take advantage of the speed of air freighting, the flow of information from the shipper's factory to the ultimate distribution point has to be completely up to date so that no time is lost in freight booking, forwarding, and receiving between stations in widely disparate countries. Consequently, only those who have been able to combine their knowledge of carrier and customs requirements with the development of sophisticated integrated systems of data processing and communications and seen themselves in the business of logistics management rather than in freight forwarding have prospered with the growth of international trade whilst old firms which failed to modernize have gone to the wall.

In the years ahead, the opening of the doors of insurance to private sector and foreign operators will once again provide to the young Indian a career opportunity which was prevalent before nationalization. Today's crop will be better suited to the job with the acquisition of tools and techniques developed since in the competitive consumer economy in which they grew up and live, and their generally global outlook.

HANDLING POLITICIANS

Perhaps more than any other country, and certainly in the first four decades of this period, a prime task of the Indian manager was handling politicians. Corporate chiefs at headquarters, unit heads in the regions, commercial seniors, all had to learn the special art of handling politicians who were constantly demanding some advantage out of the organization. This could not be dealt with on a straightforward confrontation basis but had to be tactfully handled with the least compromise of principles and without detriment to the company's future. The worst situation arose in the context of donations at election time, when practically everybody had to succumb in the seventies. This presure has created the position of a manager whose job profile consists almost exclusively of liasing with politicians. Many companies that have problems in adequately placing old, experienced executives who are for some reason or the other unable to keep pace with the requirements of altered conditions of business, have found it appropriate to utilize their knowledge of the company and their proven loyalty in making them front men in dealing with politicians.

OWNER MANAGER

No discussion of modern management in India can be complete without considering the owner manager. When talking about managers one tends to consider only the professional who seeks a career by joining an employer. In India one must also make special mention of the owner manager—perhaps more appropriately, sons of owners operating as managers.

Comment has already been made on the fact that the dominant shareholding in the Indian corporate sector is extensively in the hands of capitalist families. In the West, ownership by and large is diffused and there is no automatic career path for the children of company chiefs in their parents' organizations. In India not only is this a common factor but with the acquisition by traders and capitalists generally of foreign companies through the sixties and seventies and the tendency towards conglomeration, instances of sons of entrepreneurs joining parents' organizations are abundant.

In the beginning, there was a lot of maladjustment with the entrenched professionals. The oldtimers were already there when callow youths, untutored in the ways of modern business, started throwing their weight around. With time, however, the situation has completely changed. Sons of entrepreneurs, especially in the more established companies, are more often than not trained in elite management institutions of this country and abroad. They are inducted into organizations in a planned manner and career paths are carefully worked out so that at a later stage in family succession the empire can be divided without heartburn. Through their training and due to the wisdom and example of parents they know how to respect senior colleagues and make the best use of them.

Even where the young entrant in question has not been to a management college, he has grown up in an atmosphere of sophisticated professional management. His schoolmates, his friends in clubs, have influenced him to use his authority with discretion. His constant interaction in trade associations and similar bodies with sophisticated leaders of commerce and industry, has rounded off his own training.

When previously professionally managed companies were being taken over by Indian management there was a great deal of consternation amongst the professional management cadre about its own position. There were certainly many cases of unhappy adjustments in the first phase but today an aspiring professional does not get baulked by the fact that the company he is going to join or is working in is under owner management, so to speak. He knows his own position in the company will be safeguarded and his status in the outside world unaffected. There are many examples of presidentships of chambers of commerce and industry and trade associations where a professional from an owner-managed company has been elected . The presidentship of the high powered Confederation of Indian Industries(CII) has gone to a senior manager of the Thapar Group, several of R.P. Goenka's men have become president of the Bengal Chamber of Commerce, on many occasions the ITA has had a president from the groups run by B.M. Khaitan or G.P. Goenka. These are some of the compensations for accepting the fact that he will never be chief of the group.

At the same time ambition has to be realistic. It is true one cannot hope to be the Chief Executive Officer of the group but it is quite significant how this desire can be sublimated with careful handling by the owner's family and perceived prestige in the outside world. An effective manager or an effective specialist is highly rated as such and retained through fostering his self-esteem, using his talents, projecting him suitably to the outside world, and, of course, through abundant remuneration. He is often made chief executive of a company in the group and is accordingly 'number one' in the eyes of the outside world although within the firm a scion of the owner's family may ultimately be calling the shots.

There are, of course, plenty of examples of unsuitable, arrogant, ill-equipped offspring of owners joining companies to the detriment of the organizations' morale and performance. This is more so in families without a tradition of organized business. However, it may be observed that whatever may have happened in the beginning, after India's maturity in the industrial scene in, say, the last quarter of this century, traditional businessmen's families have been able to induct their offsprings in an acceptable manner in their empires. They have taken care of the consolidation of the core businesses and moved on to new enterprises providing a high quality of management themselves and recruiting suitably with the experience gathered in the parent organization. The group's reputation has ensured the willingness of competent, experienced professionals to join.

The professional manager himself branching out into becoming an entrepreneur is also a common feature now, particularly in the fields of consultancy, information technology, and others where relatively small capital investment is necessary and experience and brainpower are the greater assets. Very often the promoter is working in concert with fellow professionals and ex-colleagues. The actual record of their staying together, even in growth, is so far impressive.

EIGHT

A Representative First Eleven

One effective way to appreciate the actual achievements of Indian management in the half century since Independence is to have a close look at some of the men who bestrode the period from being young entrants to becoming corporate chiefs. In 1989 I was associated with such an exercise where a close look at the motivation of some of the more successful managers was sought.[1] A lot was being written about the social history of Indian management, its problems, processes, methods, and techniques. What was necessary was to record the beliefs, feelings, and perceptions of some of the men who shaped the managerial edifice of this country. Professional management had got established in India as a leading career. What was necessary now was to understand whether there would be a continuity in the values of professional managers. The study was not about achievement and career successes. It was a record of the guiding principles and thoughts of men who were acknowledged to have become leaders.

[1] *Belief and Experience.* Calcutta: UCS Consultancy, 1989.

Some two hundred managers at various levels were interviewed in order to obtain recommendations for names to appear in the list. An amazing feature was that nine of the eleven who were finally selected were on *everybody's* list. The two who were not so commonly supported were picked for special reasons—one brought in the aspect of management education and the other grew up entirely abroad and began his career at the headquarters of an MNC whose Indian outfit he was to later head.

The list of the eleven managers is given in the Appendix to this chapter, along with a thumbnail sketch of their careers up to 1989. Since then, with the exception of one, they have all moved on—through death and retirement.

They represented many different facets, providing as comprehensive a coverage as one could have hoped for. Six of them could essentially be considered to be products of private sector industry, one from the public sector, one from the cooperative movement, two from the world of high finance, and one, although he had headed major companies in both the public and private sectors, was better known for his contribution to management education. Six of them were groomed by MNCs, four had degrees in technology, and two had qualified as accountants. All had had good education without being consistently brilliant. One secured a doctorate and three others were awarded doctorates *honoris causa.* Two of them were drop-outs, so to speak, from the government's pool of scientists. Between them, in their origins they covered eight states of India. Through them one encompasses experience in steelmaking, heavy engineering, financing, consumer goods, pharmaceuticals, hotels, chemical engineering, housing, and dairy management.

Each person in his extramural capacity contributed sub-

stantially to the country's planning process, technical education, or organization of sporting and cultural activities. Two
at least were writers of distinction in their own rights on
other than professional subjects—one traced the development of his state and society through one hundred years of
British rule by looking at his own roots and the other wrote
plays which were staged on Broadway.

It would be fair to say that very few countries, if any,
could have boasted such many-splendoured qualities
amongst its top managers. It is equally true that it would
have been difficult to point to any other profession in this
country whose leaders collectively have had such a wide-
ranging impact on society at large.

The most heartening feature is that all these men entered
industry on their own qualifications and not through
backing. A critic might point out an exception or two but it
is nevertheless true that all obtained their entries through
open, objective methods and at relatively humble levels in
the organization. They worked their way up as they
established themselves. Some could even have been
considered rank outsiders for the top job. One joined, for
example, at 27 as research assistant in the laboratories of
a giant consumer goods manufacturing and marketing
company, and then becoming its Chairman in eighteen
years; another got a technical diploma while working and
rose to head a giant electrical manufacturing company.

The study was not in the realm of biographies but by
highlighting the philosophies, beliefs, and convictions of
people who had made a significant contribution to the
society in which they moved, it aimed to provide some guide
to what was still in India a relatively new career path.

A common thread runs through the stories of all the men.

They had abiding faith in the people who worked for them and in their different ways went about developing talent from within the organization. In rare instances, they resorted to importing talent at senior levels. Concern for the upliftment of the economic standard of the general population and the need for ensuring social justice were deeply rooted in all of them. They were, however, practical and confined themselves to what was achievable by their own efforts, that is simply ensuring the continued success and growth of their own organizations. At least two of them founded new organizations which remain the pride of Indian business.

The interesting feature is that in their youths, at the point they entered industry, none of these men was fired by notions of dedication or altruism. They went into whatever organization they joined, essentially because a job was being offered and the prospects seemed good—even if the job had nothing to do with their training, like a nuclear physics man going to a dairy cooperative. It speaks volumes not just for the quality of the men themselves but for the healthy ambience of the corporate world and its role in the national scene that by the time they attained recognition and their towering heights on the managerial ladder each one had developed a value system linked to a regard for fellow humans and concern for the administration of social justice. They may have, in a big majority, voiced their objections to excessive interference by the government in the running of business but these were points of dispute only on the means because with the country's developmental aims and objectives they were completely in tune.

A successful industry leader has to be pragmatic—that is almost axiomatic. An impractical idealist cannot succeed in the complexities of current-day business but mere pragmatism without being anchored in a value system in which one has firm belief and which defines the scope of what is desirable and must be made possible would be rudderless. Pragmatism in the ultimate analysis can be said to be an attempt to balance non-complementary forces and if some of the forces to be balanced were those that were strong enough to assert themselves, the weak, the uncommitted, and the unorganized would necessarily have gone to the wall.

'Excellence' is a term that is often bandied these days in the corporate world. In their approach to the subject researchers tend invariably to confuse or at least equate *managerial* excellence with *corporate* excellence. The men studied, of course, all ran organizations claiming excellence and their own contribution to the achievement of that excellence was incontrovertible; but this particular exercise took a different approach. It tried to separate the men from their achievements and get them to express themselves in a manner which led the researcher to the inner resources which manifested themselves in their pursuit of excellence.

These pioneers, along with many other pioneers of Indian professional management, had the crucial ability to realize that they were playing a significant role in the economic development of the country; that the task would grow progressively more complex and there would, therefore, be the imperative of attracting to the folds of industry the best talents of the Indian education system. They also realized that in India professionals had traditionally earned respect in society at large only if they seemed to base themselves on the systematic acquisition of knowledge in an academic sense.

By accident or by design the success of that aspiration was fantastic. Within two decades unquestionably the best talents of Indian colleges, including technological colleges, were clamouring to become professional managers. The young management trainee in industry was being held in the same regard by society as in a previous generation had the young ICS officer or the England-returned young barrister or doctor but never the business manager.

A common feature of the men studied was their cosmopolitanism—whatever professional management in India might have achieved or failed to achieve, it must without doubt be accredited with the promotion of pan-Indianism. By moving in their postings from one state to another, in frequently making business travels throughout India, they were above narrow provincialism and were truly secular. This is all the more remarkable because in their private lives they formed part of a society where narrow, reactionary forces undoubtedly held sway.

The study was truly representative of successful Indian management at the time. Favouritism, nepotism, corruption —all the banes which besmirch the image of business—had no place in their success. Values remained important as they ought to be in any honourable profession.

The broadly common denominators from the career profiles of these exemplary managers may be summed up to a thumbnail sketch of a successful corporate chief of the seventies and eighties. A fairly high level of education was a prerequisite. His job was not acquired through influence and he worked his way up the ladder. His abilities were spotted fairly early. He did not go job hopping and was on the whole satisfied with the organization he worked for. He developed a passionate commitment to corporate efficiency corporate efficiency and growth and did not view serving an MNC negatively. Indeed, he saw the great contribution that the MNC could play in the development of the nation's economy. He was a frank critic of the government's policy whenever he felt it contrary to the firm's interest and by extension the economy's; but he was disciplined enough to abide by the laws and regulations of the government. His involvement with politics was minimal although personally, as an intelligent citizen, he had his views. The welfare of his employees was a major concern and all the men listed had an excellent record in employee relations. As he attained seniority he actively engaged in extramural work which had relevance to the organization—government committees, management education, chambers of commerce—but did so without adversely affecting the performance of his own employer organization. For him to succeed in this direction required a well-primed structure run by competent deputies. When the time came for him to lay down office a worthy successor was ready (even in the much discussed Mody affair where the problem was with the person's determined opposition to retiring—a rather one-off peculiar situation—the organization had a ready successor).

Appendix to Chapter 8

Prakash L. Tandon

Born 1911; educated at the Punjab and Manchester universities. Qualified as a Fellow, Institute of Chartered Accountants, England and Wales, 1937.

Joined Lever Brothers in India in 1937. Chairman of Hindustan Lever (HLL) 1961–88. Chairman of the State Trading Corporation (STC) 1968–72 and Punjab National Bank 1972–5. Has been Chairman or Director of a large number of public and private sector companies and President of the Board of Governors of the National Council of Applied Economic Research. Has always taken keen interest in professional education by serving on the governing bodies of the Administrative Staff College of India (ASCI), Hyderabad, the Indian Institute of Teachnology (IIT), Kharagpur, the Xavier Labour Research Institute (XLRI), Jamshedpur, and the Senate of Goa University. He played an important part in the founding of IIM, Ahmedabad, of which he was Chairman from 1964 to 1970.

A prolific and pathbreaking writer, he was awarded the D.Litt *honoris causa* by the Punjab University. His writings include *Punjabi Century 1857-1947, Beyond Punjab 1937–1960, Return to Punjab 1961-1975, Punjabi Saga 1857-1987.*

Recipient of the Sir Jehangir Ghandy Gold Medal for Industrial Peace and ISA-Khatau Gold Medal of the Indian Society of Advertising.

Hashmukh T. Parekh

Born 1911; graduation in Economics in India and in Banking and Finance from the London School of Economics; qualified as a chartered accountant.

Began his career as a lecturer in economics at St Xavier's College, Bombay, and then moved on to stockbroking. In 1956, joined the newly formed Industrial Credit and Investment Corporation of India (ICICI) as Deputy General Manager and was Chairman from 1976 to 1978. Promoted Housing Development Finance Corporation Ltd, served on a number of company Boards, and was President of the Social Service League.

Had always taken keen interest in broader issues of monetary and fiscal policies and had specialized in development finance, industrial finance, and the capital market in India and abroad. Had a number of publications in English and Gujarati concerning banking, development, and entrepreneurship.

H.T. Parekh died in 1995

Rustomji Hormusji (Russi) Mody

Born 1918; educated at Harrow and Christ Church, Oxford. Worked his way up from traineeship to become Chairman and Managing Director of the Tata Iron and Steel Company Limited and Director of a number of companies.

Was Chairman of the Board of Governors of IIT, Kharagpur and of XLRI, Jamshedpur.

Has done a lot for the promotion of sports in India and was Chairman of the Finance Commission of the Indian Olympic Association.

Selected 'Businessman of the Year' in 1984 by *Business India*. Recipient of the fellowship of the Duke of Edinburgh's award. Was conferred an Award by the Indian Chamber of Commerce for promoting the cause of national integration.

Has featured amongst the six top industrial personalities of the world chosen by the BBC for their TV series entitled 'Money Makers' which has subsequently been published as a book.

Nripendra Prasanna (Potla) Sen

Born 1920; graduated from Presidency College, Calcutta. Joined the Imperial Tobacco Company Ltd in 1940; left as General Marketing Manager in 1963 to be Chairman of Vazir Sultan Tobacco Co. Ltd. In 1966 moved over to the public sector as Managing Director of the Food Corporation of India (FCI). From 1969 to 1979 was Principal of ASCI. While holding this position he was also for three years Chairman of the Indian Airlines Corporation.

Joined the Commonwealth Secretariat in London from 1979 to 1982 as Director for Human Resource Development. Was Chairman of Clarion Advertising and Director of several public sector companies.

N.P. Sen died in 1995.

Verghese Kurien

Born in 1921; educated at Madras University (B.Sc. and B.E.) Stumbled quite accidentally into dairy engineering through which he and Kaira or Anand in Gujarat became world famous.

Chairman of the Gujarat Co-operative Milk Marketing Federation, the National Dairy Development Board, the Institute of Rural Management, and the National Co-operative Dairy Federation of India.

Has been lauded with honours both in India and abroad including, among others, the Ramon Magsaysay Award for Community Leadership in 1963, the Padma Bhusan in 1966, an Honorary Doctorate in Science from Michigan and in Law from Glasgow. In 1989 received the World Food Prize for his cooperative programme, Operation Flood, on milk distribution all over India.

All Kurien's work has essentially centred around the upliftment of the rural sector and the quality of its life largely through the cooperative movement.

Ajit Narain Haksar

Born 1925; educated at Doon School, Allahabad University and Harvard Business School.

After a brief stint with J. Walter Thompson in New York, joined Imperial Tobacco Co. (which later became ITC Ltd.) in 1948 as a 'Pupil' and rose to be its Chairman from 1969 to 1983. On retirement he was given the unique honour of being made Chairman Emeritus. During his tenure he transformed the character of the exclusively tobacco manufacturing foreign-controlled company to one of India's largest multipurpose corporate entities. Has been associated with many public and private sector boards and was President of the Associated Chambers of Commerce.

Has served on the Board of Governors of Doon School and the ASCI. Was Chairman of IIT, Kharagpur, the Indian School of Mines, and a member of the Council of Jawaharlal Nehru University, amongst other academic management involvements.

His many awards include *Business India's* first 'Businessman of the Year', induction into the *Business World's* Hall of Fame and, Udyog Rattan of the Institute of Economic Studies.

V. Krishnamurthy

Born 1925. Has been Chairman of Bharat Heavy Electricals (BHEL), Maruti Udyog Ltd, and the Steel Authority of India Limited (SAIL). Was Secretary, Department of Heavy Industry, Government of India, from 1977 to 1981.

Was the Chairman of IIM, Bangalore and IIM, Ahmedabad.

Was chosen 'Businessman of the Year 1987' by *Business India* and was the recipient of the Tata Gold Medal for significant contributions to the metallurgical industry, and the Sir Jehangir Ghandy Gold Medal for Industrial Peace.

Was awarded D.Litt. *honoris causa* by Pondicherry University the Padma Shri in 1973, and the Padma Bhushan in 1986 for his contribution to public management.

T. Thomas

Born 1927; graduated as a Chemical Engineer.

Worked as an industrial engineer consultant from 1950 to 1954. Joined HLL in 1954 which he left in 1964 to be Technical Director of Madras Rubber Factory (MRF). Rejoined HLL in 1966 as General Factory Manager, Bombay. Promoted to the Board of HLL in 1968 and became Chairman in 1973. Joined the Board of Unilever PLC London and Unilever NV Rotterdam in 1979. On retirement was Chairman of Sandoz and Glaxo in India.

Suresh S. Nadkarni

Born 1934; graduated in mechanical engineering and started his career in the field of industrial engineering and business consultancy. Joined the Industrial Credit and Investment Corporation of India (ICICI) in 1960 in a junior management position and rose through the ranks rapidly to be its Chairman and Managing Director in January 1984. In 1985, he took charge of the country's apex development banking institution, the Industrial Development Bank of India (IDBI), as Chairman and Managing Director.

Was awarded the Business Leadership Award in 1987 and received the Padma Bhusan in 1989.

S.S. Nadkarni died, prematurely, in 1994.

Ashok S. Ganguly

Born 1935; graduated from Bombay University and received his MS and Ph.D. from the University of Illinois, USA.

Joined HLL as a management trainee in 1962 and worked as a scientist in its Research Division in India, UK, the Netherlands, and the USA for nearly a decade. Joined the Board of HLL as

Technical Director in 1977 and was Chairman from 1980.

Played a significant role in the national scene on technical education and R.&D. matters. Was Chairman of the Board of Governors of IIT Kanpur, a member of the Scientific Advisory Council to the Prime Minister, a member of the Council of Scientific and Industrial Research (CSIR), and a member of the Indian & US Councils for the Programme for the Advancement of Commercial Technology. Was also Member on the Committee of Capital Issues (Control) Act, Government of India, and a member of the Company Law Advisory Committee. Was on the Governing Body of the ASCI and the National Council of Applied Economic Research.

Was selected as the Businessman of the Year in 1986 by *Business India*. Received the Padma Bhusan.

Gurcharan Das

Born 1943; graduated from Harvard University.

Joined Vicks in America at 20 with the main object of returning to India. Became a marketing trainee with Vicks, India, from December 1963 and became President and Managing Director of the successor company, Procter and Gamble.

Has authored several plays which have been successfully produced and published. *Larins Sahib*, a prize-winning play about the British in India, was produced in Bombay and by the BBC in London and published by Oxford University Press in England. *Mira* (on singer Saint Mirabai) was staged on Broadway to critical acclaim. A Spanish version was performed in Mexico City and Madrid. Has also published a novel about an Indian family.

Presently works as a management consultant.

NINE

In a Changing Society

A manager is not an island unto himself; he is very much a part of society. His early upbringing, influenced certainly by society and his environment, moulds him. An understanding of his way of functioning is, therefore, incomplete without a comprehension of his place in society.

The managers in the first part of the period under review came from a fairly restricted class background which can broadly be described as 'upper middle class'. In the ultimate analysis, the intrinsic values were common although due to geography, religion, and relative family affluence, there would have been variations on the surface. They were the products of privileged families in a colonial society. This privilege did not necessarily mean contacts and influence in the right quarters—although in many cases that too existed—but a certain edge in primary and secondary education (notably in English medium schools), urbanity, and a common attitude towards discretionary expenditure. They had membership of clubs which operated on firm principles of exclusivity. Directly or indirectly they were imbued with an inherited spirit of the struggle for independence although very few of the families had directly participated in that movement. At the same time, they had deep admiration for the competence, achievements, and democratic processes of the British. Their concerns were fashioned in a milieu where the preponderant middle and lower middle classes had not been consciously using the political powers with which they had been progressively empowered and were still subservient in nature.

Their entry and growth in management took place in the era dominated by Nehru where their own value systems were basically in consonance with the ideals of the state The primary task before the nation was believed to be the upliftment of the economy and of the poor of the country, and the Indian manager shared such beliefs although he may not have stirred too actively to serve. However, as indeed with the government, progress began to be measured in purely quantitative, statistical terms and the lack of qualitative progress did not seem to bother anyone. As long as one honestly believed that one was doing a job which increased production and productivity for the country and provided the government with sufficient revenue to meet Plan objectives, in whatever sector that might be, there was a sense of personal achievement, and there was no occasion for guilt. It is true that the growing strength of trade union organizations jarred this complacency from time to time but even trade union demands were countered by well-defined parameters of comparison through the region-cum-industry principle; there was not felt any great need to go beyond the immediate demands to prepare for the shifting trends in the masses. From time to time professional institutes like the Ahmedabad Textile Industry Research Association (ATIRA) might have come out with incisive studies but as with many such exercises in different directions, the theory, however relevant hardly ever made any impact on practitioners or was considered fit for application in their own spheres. About rural India constituting 70 per cent of the population there was little concern and even rural marketing existed only in seminar discussions. All this while the poor from villages were pouring into cities expanding them with slums and shanties of which no account was taken although they would provide the next batch of recruits into factories.

The first two decades, therefore, were a relatively stable period for Indian management. As already commented upon, the task at hand was to establish management as a profession, gain for it the respect that society accorded any of the established professions, promote management education as an end in itself, and generally ensure acceptable results from one's own organization.

The winds of change that had begun to blow from the period and gained intensity after the departure of Nehru caught Indian management up in quantum changes and produced a destabilization factor with which it has only just begun to cope.

In the first place, the public sector had become by far the major employer of managers. As a result of government policy, the numbers involved, and strong regional pulls public sector management began to be filled with young men who did not conform to the prevailing recruitment standards for private sector managers. Those in power in the public sector appreciated this and spent profusely on formal management education for their managers at all levels, using short- to medium-term, part-time to full-time courses. Expectedly, the results were mixed. A dominant feeling amongst the participants was that their training and job requirements were much in advance of those of their private sector counterparts who were being paid much more for less responsible jobs. This engendered a feeling of frustration which did managerial ambience little good.

By this time the country had entered a phase where the masses had begun to appreciate the power that the ballot boxes gave them. Increasingly, corporate management's ability to cope with the rising tide of demands was diminishing. Unfortunately, awareness of ballot power amongst the electorate at large coincided with the rapid erosion of the value system and the dream of a modern India which had formed the backbone of the Independence movement and continued to inspire independent India for two decaded or so. Corruption became the order of the day.

By now the numbers that the corporate sector—both public and private—needed had gone beyond the ability of the dwindling colonized class to supply. Rural wealth, success of small traders, and increasing payscales for the huge army of government Class III and IV employees were, on the other hand, generating upward social mobility and new middle classes. They were bent on removing the handicaps which had precluded them so far from seeking employment in the higher echelons of the organized sector. English was seen as an instrument of social exclusion and so English medium schools—never mind the quality— sprouted everywhere. Young men were no longer content to stay in villages and city population rose astronomically. The proximity of the privileged and their living conditions generated animosities which would have had a dangerous impact on the solidarity of the management cadre had not the proliferation of institutions providing MBAs taken place simultaneously. The state embarked on a policy of expenditure on higher education to the neglect of primary education. The new aspirants were thus acquiring degrees and diplomas all right but their fundamentals did not stand up to competition with the children of the elite and resentment abounded at work-places. The growing competitiveness of business generally was also making employers look for different values in their managerial cadre. From the fifties right through till the end-seventies it was important for senior management to be seen in social clubs and golf courses or entertain in decent homes. By the middle of the eighties these things no longer mattered in the promotion of one's career.

In society at large, the effects of the Mandal Commission and periodic emphasis on the use of Hindi had become unavoidable realities in the public sector. Private sector organizations did not have to conform to these edicts although some did try to show a measure of voluntary progress.

What, however, the private sector did have to succumb to in the selection of managers was constant pressure from a state which was frighteningly authoritative from the beginning of the seventies and later, with the disintegration of that authoritative centralism into regional power centres, pressure from regional power brokers. Recruitment standards often had to be bent. Industry bosses who had hitherto ignored state governments now began taking serious note of them.

As a part of this process of state control the major banks were nationalized and industries dealing with banks became bureaucratic. Banking was no longer seen as a source of funds where sanctions were made on the basis of the banker's judgement of the project and the ability of the borrower to deliver. One of the great pioneers of Indian banking had a favourite saying that a bank manager should sit at the end of a long narrow room and if, by the time the prospective client had walked up to his desk, he could not size him up then he was a poor banker indeed! From now on, bank loans were to be given on the basis of paperwork where consultants thrived in making the answers acceptable with not too great a respect for facts. Means of lubricating the process of sanctions became common. These were new skills which the manager had to acquire.

The lifestyle of the Indian manager has undergone profound change during the last fifty years. At the beginning there was a frank attempt to appear a special class. Salaries did not support such ambitions but perquisites did and the managerial class was by and large inbred and out of tune with the wider social environment. The extent to which this happened was brilliantly portrayed in Satyajit Ray's *Seemabaddha* (Limited Company). A successful executive madly engaged in a rat race against a particular colleague ultimately wins a promotion to the Board, the very Olympian heights to him and his wife, but in the process he becomes a person quite different from the idealistic college student and Shakespearean scholar—a person who is embarrassed by the arrival of his unsophisticated parents in the presence of his business friends. As he attains his career goal, the viewer is left with the impression that the successful executive has probably begun to question whether the prize was worth the transformation.

With the influx of the arriviste in huge numbers from

the new middle classes and the all-pervasive intrusion of electronic media into homes, the situation has altered considerably. Salaries today are practically limitless and the new breed of highly trained and highly paid information technology specialists is anxious to telescope into a few years what it feels it has been deprived of through generations. The young Indian manager is becoming detached from his own traditional and cultural links and is in a frenetic hurry to accept unthinkingly Western lifestyles (for entertainment particularly) for which his base is unprepared. As Pawan K. Varma has put it in his *The Great Indian Middle Class*.

The absence of a strong moral imperative for social altruism has resulted under the tutelage of unethical leaders and opportunistic politics in a horribly bloated unconcern for society itself. The end product is the acceptance of a certain kind of lifestyle; insular, aggressive, selfish, obsessed with material gain, and sociallly callous.

The isolation of the Indian manager from the vast millions of the underprivileged and rural population is a serious problem particularly since there seems to be no improvement in either the attitude or the distance. Western countries have the advantage of a fairly homogeneous population with a reasonable minimum standard of living. It will be a long, long time before there is such a situation in India and for its own survival and growth the management class has to be conscious about closing the 'we'—'they' gap both at the workplace and in the market at large. Till such time as India comes to occupy a respectable position in the league table of the World Development Report, management's task will remain unfulfilled.

TEN

A SWOT Analysis

In managerial jargon it may be useful at this stage to do a SWOT analysis of current day Indian managers—to list their strengths and weaknesses and analyse the opportunities they have and the threats they face as a class.

STRENGTHS

One cannot but be impressed with the personal attainments—intellectual and academic—of the Indian managerial class as a whole. This does not necessarily hold true to the same degree for their counterparts in other countries. Also, it is not asserted that such attainments are essential for managerial performance; rather it indicates the respect which the profession commands in Indian society so that the best talents look for a career in it. Indian society has always had high regard for a profession which is manifestly higher-education based. Intrinsically this calibre meets one great necessity of modern day business, particularly Indian business—the ability to cope with constant and rapid changes and adapt one's business to such changes. Experience by itself has great value but is not necessarily adjusted to tackle this rapid rate of change. This is where the education and intellectual capabilities of the Indian manager can be of help especially considering we do not have the advantage of two hundred years of managerial experience in our genes.

A particular matter of pride in this respect is that, with a few exceptions, Indian managers are totally bred in India. They are the products of Indian universities and specialist institutions who have taken up employment fresh from their educational institutions. In this, professional management is in sharp contrast with medicine or academics where foreign training still carries a premium. In fact, potential managers returning with foreign degrees find it difficult to get suitable employment and, even when employed, their foreign qualifications do not *ipso facto* carry any advantage against home bred colleagues.

In advancement to the top, the operation of meritocracy is undisputed. People who are at the top of the managerial ladder throughout India are there because they have in every way earned it. There might have been a time when 'influence' was an important factor in getting into good companies but, as remarked earlier, this had begun to die out in the sixties. Even then, for subsequent progress within the organization, merit was the sole criterion (members of owners' families were, of course, exceptions). Favouritism did operate in a few cases, it was only at a rate which was common in any country and the undeserving promotee was soon found out.

Whatever he may be in private life, the Indian manager is, by and large, truly catholic in his approach to his job. When at work he does not have to force himself to be consciously secular or cosmopolitan and takes decisions best suited to the organization's interest and at times inimical to the interests of the narrow confines of his caste, creed, or region. The proof of this statement is in the percentage of non-locals who are at the helm of organizations in our metropolitan cities. Indeed, it is often said that a manager from say Tamil Nadu or West Bengal performs much better outside his state than he would in his own. Perhaps the absence of inherited local influences sharpens objectivity. The many success stories of managers basically trained in this country's educational institutions and working in top positions abroad are another indication of the inherent strength of the background from which managers come. With racial prejudices disappearing, MNCs are now widely using managers from their Indian companies to head their operations in other countries.

The speed with which Indian managers have competently dealt with change is seen by the leap in the quality of executives in the modern-day world once the tools became accessible and opportunities became abundant. This has been seen in the speed and degree of computerization in offices; in the computer literacy which almost all levels of managers have acquired; and in the sophistication with which the money market has been tackled once liberalization brought about changes. This quality, one hopes, will be put to very good use in India's international trade which has still to take off at a rate consistent with the country's size and resources.

WEAKNESSES

The Indian manager coming as he essentially does from the middle class reflects that class's notorious lack of commitment to the community at large. Regrettably this seems to have become worse with the improvement in educational level of the intake. Also, those coming from unsophisticated and not so well-to-do backgrounds reflect a typical attitude of the class by shedding past associations and their obligations thereto. The managerial class is an important high profile section in the Indian community today. It must ask itself how long it can continue to operate effectively as an island amongst the masses of the deprived and have-nots. There are some sporadic conscience-salving efforts through Chambers of Commerce or Rotary Clubs but unless the majority of managers accept the need and devote some of their talent and resources towards enriching the immediate environment they will remain a threatened class.

Nobody will be so unfair as to lay the blame for widespread failure to tackle trade unions such as to instil meaningful messages of productivity at the door of management exclusively. Indeed, there are many wonderful examples of managerial success in harnessing worker capacity into gainful productivity on a sustained basis. Nevertheless, management's incapability to gauge the nature of workers' motivation and guide them often in an adverse situation irresponsibly created by local politicians and power brokers must, in the ultimate analysis, count as a management failure.

India may be moving towards modernity but Indian managers, by and large, have been brought up in families where there was unquestioned acceptance of parental authority. There was hardly any atmosphere at home of discussions on issues and objectives or reasoned arguments against such issues.

This is bound to have left a streak of authoritarianism in

the Indian manager who, despite all his attainments, is frontally abjectly subservient to the boss while being at best aloof and at times quite uncivil towards his subordinates. The Indian manager's style is still very much directive oriented: subordinates get used to doing what they are asked to do. Creativity and innovation suffer in consequence. Confrontation always takes on a negative connotation and is not seen as a ground for finding commonly acceptable solutions. Executive meetings are rarely used as sounding boards. That cardinal principle of management that when a decision is being formulated officers should give their frank views freely but after a decision has been arrived at all concerned should accept it without reservation rarely operates in India. Managers do not use their right to be consulted even when this opportunity is given and when the decision so formulated comes a cropper protests their previous reservations—often openly.

Indian managers come from an environment which is still heavily bureaucratic. In the public sector things may be improving now but for long anybody who took a decision without recording the reasons on paper and getting two or three other signatures ran a grave risk of jeopardizing his career. In the nationalized banks Board papers run into several volumes and each case of loan sanction is supported by at least 10–15 pages of analytical paperwork and historical background which no director possibly has the time to go through. One of the reasons for such profusion of information without an authoritative decision-announcing note is an inborn tendency to shield oneself against criticism for a decision which may later turn sour.

Even in the private sector the culture of passing instructions or communicating through memos and notes with colleagues sitting in the same office is only now dying a slow death. A false sense of prestige prevents physical circulation within the office on errands, and peons and clerks therefore proliferate. For long, the telephone system in Indian cities was in an abysmal state and business was best done by letters. Today, in the age of improved telecommunication services, fax, and e-mail the readjustment of this attitude is taking place.

A person who in the seventies took over as the Chief Executive of a very large organization just released from the control of a managing agency recalls how he made himself terribly unpopular with the seniormost management staff (most of whom had been in position for more than twenty years and drew India's top-level salaries) because, when they brought problems relating to their areas of operation to him, he listened patiently and then encouragingly asked them to take their own decisions. Life hitherto had been very simple with decisions being sought from and given by bosses in the managing agency. If things went well the departmental chief took the credit; otherwise the head office was always there to be blamed for taking uninformed, uninvolved decisions. With the younger crop of managers this tendency is now on the decline but a lot still depends on the culture of an organization.

A high cost is attached to current day salary structures. The pressures at work are generally much more intense than what new entrants faced in previous generations and these pressures remain unmitigated due to several factors. The pressure due to the accountability that is demanded today of every executive has already been mentioned. In addition, there is a great deal of competition in the executive supply market and product competition is far higher than it ever used to be. New techniques are constantly entering all areas of business activity and the dread of obsolescence is much greater leading to high degrees of stress. Again the work day is, necessarily, much longer and since in most modern marriages both partners are working, the strains of the workplace frequently cross over into the domestic sphere. The situation is exacerbated by the lack of infrastructural facilities for working parents: with the trend towards nuclear families on the rise grandparents are not always available to do babysitting and with reliable domestic help on the decline and organized, well-regulated child-care systems yet to develop, bringing up children is yet another contribution to stress. Consequently, stress management is now a common feature in management programmes.

Perhaps because of their very considerable educational attainment, and because of the lack of inherited traditions of business, Indian managers have a tendency to make things complicated and complex. One of the main reasons for this is the lack of dependence on subordinates and the inadequacy of information on which decisions are being taken. Chief Executives and other seniors rarely have high powered competent staff supports—a system which Indian corporates should seriously foster. There also seems to be a lack of ability to sift through matter to arrive at simple fundamentals. Richard Feynman should be compulsory reading for Indian managers.

An endemic problem of the Indian manager has traditionally been scant regard to details. It is ingrained in our psyche so that even the most meticulously trained engineer talks loosely in terms of 0.3mm to 0.5mm estimation of measurement. Associated with this is the trait, unnoticed by ourselves but catching the foreigner's ear, of making a definitive statement first, realizing immediately the snag, and then qualifying—'I have never been to Agra except twice'. In a managerial context it might mean that a position has been declared too soon and without much thought given from which climbing down might mean some loss of face and untenable positions might have to be expensively and unnecessarily defended. This is an aspect which will require several generations of training and self-conscious exposure to root out.

Indian managers are good doers but not necessarily great thinkers. One reason for this is the lack of dependence on subordinates and a tendency to either direct a subordinate totally or even do his job for him. Consequently, the subordinate gets inadequately trained for the promotion which will call for exercising vision: to think more about tomorrow than about today or yesterday.

The business to which Indian managers belong are riding high on the explosion of consumerism in Indian middle-class society in this decade. The lifestyle of the Indian manager himself runs the risk of being swamped by this tidal wave. One hopes the discerning Indian manager will be able to develop a value system which helps him exercise discretion in spending and savings. The signs are not too encouraging. Like most other middle class citizens pent up desires for previously unavailable consumer goods now stoked by relentless exposure to media promotions hinder the manager from exercising discretion.

OPPORTUNITIES

Opportunities naturally arise from globalization and the extension of the market from the narrow confines of the country to the world at large. Simple as it may sound, this has required complete adaptation of the mindsets of executives who grew up in three to four decades of a wholly protected and closed economy. Their concept of the economies of scale, for example, was askew. For long Indian management was used to introducing a product manufactured for the first time in India by pricing it on the basis of the prevailing landed cost. A shortage psyche with simultaneous banning of imports following local manufacture fetched handsome profits from the start if there was no mismanagement. Consequently, to get maximum benefit out of capital invested, plant size could be down scaled compared to international standards to keep unit costs of production down to a level below this high selling price after a reasonable use of capacity to ensure feeding the market. Competition was conditioned by the country's industrial licensing policy so that chances of over-production were minimized. For people trained under such conditions to look at the world market with a competitive product or face competition from freely permitted imports requires a lot of reorientation. However, the opportunities the market expansion offers are colossal provided management right down the line is geared to be cost competitive and is quality-conscious once the entrepreneur has secured level playing field with international competitors. The recent craze for total quality management (TQM) and ISO certification augurs well as long as these are not just external decorations.

In the first flush of liberalization the story used to be told of the Indian capitalist who had two plants, one in Thailand and one in India, making an identical product with an absolutely identical plant. When the Indian market began to receive the imported product at a price much lower than what had made the Indian plant's production profitable hitherto, the Indian plant faced closure. At the same time, the Chief Executive of the Thai company came to see the group Chairman with a proposal seeking capital for doubling his output. The Chairman was impressed with the project figures but asked a crucial question—where would all this additional production be marketed? The prompt answer from the visiting Chief Executive was—Why, India of course!

This incident—even if it is partly apocryphal—highlights several things. First of all it shows that we have to be cost competitive. Plants need to be based on modular concepts so that capacity can be increased at marginal capital cost to reduce the unit cost of production. There can be no cutting down on quality and the global market and global product development need to be continuously scanned.

However, the possibility of a completely different opportunity is thrown up in this particular case. If imports are that much cheaper and cannot, on reasonable capital investment, be countered with local manufacture is there much point in continuing with the manufacture of this product? Here again a particular generation is incapable of thinking in terms of importing something by stopping local manufacture. The success of Japan as an industrial nation is studied by all management institutes and the social engineering following the Meiji restoration, the discipline of the workforce, and national character are all regarded as having contributed to this twentieth-century miracle. What, however, has not been given due importance and which was also crucial to Japan's economic success was the negotiating skill that the Japanese developed for international trade. For a country which does not have its own iron ore, coal, or limestone sources to even plan to be a major steel

producer was a remarkable exercise displaying the competence with which imports could be organized and could remain consistently competitive as the tremendous sustained
growth of the Japanese steel industry through the century
has demonstrated.

This is an area of opportunity to which Indian management having shed the inhibitions of a protected market must
turn. To a class which has shown remarkable intellectual
powers and adaptability, developing negotiating skills in the
world market should come naturally provided it is seen as
an opportunity. India is blessed with enormous and varied
resources and its reach does not need to remain confined
to local availability and local markets.

Exports have suffered all these years because they have
been provided with struts instead of being looked at as a
natural outlet. This was partly due to lack of experience in
international trading but more particularly due to a mistaken
belief that special facilities would have to be created for
exports. Any manager familiar with the running of a factory
would know that it is not possible to gear the men and
machines to ensure superb quality for exports one day and
an indifferent product for the domestic market the next.
With the tremendous growth of purchasing power of what
is described arguably as the world's largest middle class
managers should seize the opportunity to produce world
class quality for the home market and expand it to the extent
that the economies of scale make export pricing competitive
and the product does not need to be propped up with
subsidies for sale abroad. Exporters of frozen marine
products are free to import flexible packaging from
anywhere in the world. Yet in displays in frozen food
counters abroad Indian products can be identified from a

distance by their shoddiness even as compared to the products of our neighbouring countries.

Now that India has opened its markets and an insatiable consumer class is demanding quality products for which it is prepared to pay, home quality should equal world quality. Exports will then happen naturally provided our costs aided by a weak rupee match and we know how to market abroad.

The intimate knowledge of the global situation should provide untold opportunities as long as the Indian manager is not just familiar with what is going on but tries to see in each situation an opportunity for the country. For example, when America talks about restricting the employment of computer operators from India one should immediately see in this an opportunity to get American business with software establishments in India with telelink facilities leading into the client's computers, thus providing the client with the cheapest possible solution to his needs.

Indeed, the software is an area with endless opportunities for which the country has an enormous reservoir of talent. Our strength should be seen as lying in our brain power and with the shifting of the world's leading economies from manufacturing to information and services technology, it should be possible now to do business with limited application of financial capital. Never before was there such opportunity in such scope for the Indian professional class.

Threats

The threats for which management needs to be prepared should also be studied. With the loosening of the tight controls of the Company Law Department much more frequent changes of corporate ownership and corporate mergers will be seen. This is a hazard which management in every developing nation faces regularly but in India we have still to reach a point where there is a tradition of management, a certain consistency of approach by different owners, and an in-built respect for management in the owner's style of operation.

The financial institutions which hold clout-giving percentage of shares in companies generally need to be activated to ensure that there is no destabilization of professionally well-managed companies by change of ownership and to have a fair assessment of the credentials of the aspiring new owner. The abdication of this role by the financial institutions in several companies at critical junctures when untested predators were trying to gain control has led to results which are only too painfully well known.

Professional management *per se* must be able to generate a greater acceptance of its role in the success of organizations. It is a little surprising that Indian management has not produced an apex organization which is regarded as a natural consulting body by policy-makers in this country. The wholly modern and professional look which the Confederation of Indian Industries (CII), has brought into the Indian business scene after years of indifferent and somewhat routine interaction by the major Chambers of Commerce with such policy makers is an eye-opener to what it is possible to achieve. The All India Management Association (AIMA), which had a head start in the matter has become a bureaucratic paper-producing body which has made little impact either on policy makers or on the development of managerial excellence. The office bearers elected from year to year are not by any means the biggest names in the Indian management world or even the heads of their own organizations. The AIMA runs seminars and produces pamphlets but is not a vibrant body with a major role of influence-moulding in matters with which it is concerned in the same way as say the British Institute of Management. For that matter there is no active Institute of Directors either in this country where the non-owning executive directors can articulate their beliefs drawing a parallel once again with the Institute of Directors, UK.

As remarked earlier, India has a preponderance of owner managers and we will see more and more well-trained sons and daughters of capitalists who do not necessarily have exposure to professional management taking over organizations. Indian professional management needs to develop a strategy for dealing with this, beginning with ensuring that the professional manager's views are regarded with respect.

In the ultimate analysis, however, the big threat is one of demography. China has set a spectacular growth rate. It would appear that this growth is entirely confined to the two hundred million or so who live along the eastern seaboard and the powers that be are not over-concerned with the remaining eight hundred million. China still possesses a totalitarian central authority to see such discriminatory policy consciously through and the physical separation of the risingly affluent from the statically non-affluent can be kept safeguarded.

In India the way things are going we will have a similar situation where say two hundred million people will reach unprecedented heights of affluence but the country's poor will remain poor and will multiply greatly. Unfortunately, such separation as occurs in China is not feasible in India. There will, therefore, be islands of affluence in the midst of seas of poverty. Whether one can continue politically to cope with this situation without destabilization is a matter of conjecture and will require great political acumen since the have-nots today appreciate the power they can exercise through the ballot box.

This is a threat which management must recognize and take concerted action to deal with for its own survival. Management is in an eminent position to do this—by the strength of its numbers, by its geographical dispersion, by its need to develop the economy beyond the middle class and to operate with a smooth infrastructure. What is necessary is consciousness and acceptance of the problem. For this to happen as has already been stated, the manager's roots amongst the people must not be severed but nurtured to understand thoughts and reactions. The urban working class and staff constitute a large and important section of the urban population. It is also hoped that sooner rather than later penetration of the rural market by consumer goods and services will motivate discerning managers to create general awareness of the beneficial effects of a good management on the economy and the value of stability.